Menu for Mom ♥

Wine: Rosé de Provence

Artichokes with Mustard Sauce
~
Lemon Sole with Butter and Capers
~
Garlic Spinach with Croutons
~
Salade Vinaigrette
~
Shorey's Raspberry Cake

A Grandfather's Lessons

A Grandfather's Lessons
In the Kitchen with Shorey

Jacques Pépin

Photographs by Tom Hopkins

Illustrations by Jacques Pépin

A RUX MARTIN BOOK

Houghton Mifflin Harcourt   Boston • New York • 2017

Library of Congress Cataloging-in-Publication Data
Names: Pépin, Jacques, author.
Title: A grandfather's lessons : in the kitchen with Shorey / Jacques Pépin;
photographs by Tom Hopkins.
Description: Boston : Houghton Mifflin Harcourt, [2017] | Includes index.
Description based on print version record and CIP data provided by publisher;
resource not viewed.
Identifiers: LCCN 2017010371 (print) | LCCN 2017011265 (ebook) | ISBN
    9780544824393 (paper over board) | ISBN 9780544824409 (ebook)
Subjects: LCSH: Cooking. | Fathers and daughters. | LCGFT: Cookbooks.
Classification: LCC TX714 (ebook) | LCC TX714.P4535 2017 (print) | DDC
    641.5—dc23
LC record available at https://lccn.loc.gov/2017010371

Book design by Endpaper Studio

Printed in China
SCP 10 9 8 7 6 5 4 3 2 1

To my son-in-law, Rollie, and all fathers
who cook with their daughters to create unique
and unforgettable memories

Acknowledgments

LIKE MOST OF MY BOOKS, *A Grandfather's Lessons* originated in our daily life. I've been cooking in the kitchen with my granddaughter, Shorey, since she was about six years old, showing her how to make chocolate truffles—since she, like most children, loves chocolate—and answering questions she asked about cooking, life, and school. We always have fun being together, cooking together, spending time together.

So we continued going to the garden, to the beach, picking wild leeks and mushrooms, collecting eggs directly from the chickens, and going to the market. She enjoyed all things associated with cooking and had a great time, as I did. Eventually, when she appeared on one of my shows, I realized that, like her mother (but unlike her grandmother!), she was very comfortable on television.

One thing led to another, and I finally said, "Why don't we write a book showing the relationship between a grandfather and a granddaughter and how it can be enhanced and made better by spending time together in the kitchen? Why not film some 8- to 10-minute shows together that demonstrate simple recipes and the fun of cooking together?" At some point, Shorey started drawing in her book of menus at home and in mine. She loves to paint and draw, and this became part of her tradition. Of course,

just like any book, *A Grandfather's Lessons* needed a lot of coordinating and a lot of help to accomplish.

I want to thank my wife, Gloria, for putting up with us in the kitchen; Claudine for helping advise Shorey and directing her; and my son-in-law, Rollie, to whom I have dedicated this book in appreciation for his enthusiasm for the project and his love, ideas, and help in the kitchen when we taped or took pictures for this book and the videos.

I thank Norma Galehouse, my assistant of more than thirty years, for helping me put yet another book together and for her good-natured help.

I certainly want to thank Tom Hopkins a great deal for his friendship and photographic sensibility and for shooting hundreds and hundreds of pictures of Shorey and me cooking or just having fun together. I'm also grateful for his good ideas for the project and for working on the filming of the video segments to go with some of the recipes. I want to thank Rich Kosenski, who assisted Tom during the photo sessions.

Thank you to Sur La Table for sponsoring the video lessons, which express more than just the recipes themselves and help demonstrate the relationship between Shorey and me. Thanks, too, to Pete and Chris, for their video expertise.

I thank Rux Martin, my editor, for her confidence in and help with the project. Thanks, too, to Doe Coover, my agent, who, as always, was very involved and had great ideas for the production of the book as well as the videos.

More than anyone else, of course, I thank my coworker, my grand-daughter, Shorey, for her love, her kindness, and for working with me so well. Shorey likes to draw, as I do, and she helped me with the illustrations for the book and the choice of drawings. She made me look terrific! I love her, and this book will cement our love even more.

Finally, my gratitude to everyone involved in the production of this book or the television segments. I'm grateful for your help and your dedication.

"The best meal I've ever had happens almost every day. A homemade meal with fresh, organic ingredients shared by family and friends."
—Shorey

Contents

Introduction

I HAVE ALWAYS COOKED FOR MY FAMILY. Even when I was a child, I cooked with my mother or for her or for my brothers or my father—and later on, for my wife, Gloria, and for my daughter, Claudine. I held Claudine in my arms when she was a couple of years old and let her stir the soup pot or mix the salad. She would get all excited and insist that she had "made it," and she could not wait to taste it. It was her production. It is important to have a child spend time in the kitchen—the most secure, comfortable, loving place in the house. The smell of food cooking, your mother's or father's voice, the clang of the utensils, and the taste of the food: These memories will stay with you for the rest of your life. The purpose of this simple book about cooking with Shorey, my granddaughter, is to show how spending time together in the kitchen can enhance your life as well as your relationship.

My cooking has changed a great deal in the last thirty years, but regardless of the style or the food, traditions remain important at our house. Sitting down together for dinner is an essential part of our daily life. In this book, I wanted to cook things with my granddaughter that she likes, and I also wanted to teach her easy, logical steps that she could understand. I wanted to prepare food that is simple but elegant, and, more than anything, I wanted it to be fun. I have always liked to simplify the steps of

1

cooking to get to the essentials, and I always place more emphasis on taste than on presentation. I wanted Shorey to tell me, "Papi, this is really good!" Like most children, she is very honest—if she likes something, she tells you; if she doesn't, she tells you that as well.

Shorey is precocious in her food tastes, which is understandable, considering that her father, Rollie, is a chef and her mother, my daughter, Claudine, cooks every day for the family, using the best and freshest possible food available, either from their garden or from organic markets nearby. When she was about two years old, I asked Shorey if she liked blueberries. She responded, "Oh, yes, I love blueberries. They have a lot of antioxidants in them." *I* barely knew that word! She is precocious, curious, and inquisitive. From the age of five, whenever she came to our house, she liked to stand next to me at the counter on an upside-down wooden box so she could "help" me cook. She would do small jobs, like wash the lettuce, pass me the ingredients or tools, or go into the garden with me to pick herbs that she would taste and help me clean.

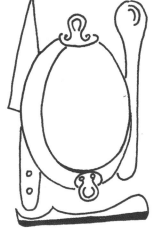

Shorey is a gourmand and eats almost everything because, just as it was with Claudine when she was a child, her parents don't give her a choice: Dinner comes to the table, and whether it is spinach, string beans, squash, tomatoes, poultry, or fish, that is dinner. So she grew up loving artichokes, Brussels sprouts, and spinach, just as Claudine did. I think it is a mistake to feed children something other than what is on the family menu or to reward them for eating spinach or Brussels sprouts. There are exceptions, of course. I know Shorey is not crazy about my tripe and headcheese, but that's okay; I know that eventually that will change. What is important is to put the meal on the table and engage in conversation while enjoying it.

For this book, I wanted to feature dishes that Shorey would have fun making. For example, my Curly Dogs with Pickle Relish (page 90) demonstrated a way of cutting hot dogs so they curl. She likes fish, so we made Salmon for Grandma (page 76), as well as Lemon Sole with Butter and Lemon (page 70), which she prepares with her mother. Sometimes we enjoyed just eating radishes and butter in the French way (see Radis au Beurre, page 17). We created a kind of dressing called *mayogrette*, a mixture of vinaigrette and mayonnaise, that we used to dress a potato salad (see page 39). We also made Garlic Spinach with Croutons (page 135), which she adores, and Mashed Potatoes with Garlic (page 132). Like me, Shorey loves pasta, so we prepared Macaroni, Spinach, and Ham Gratin (page 114) and Bow-Tie Pasta in Garden Vegetable Sauce (page 110). She had a blast making a big one-dish meal of Sausage, Potatoes, Onions, and Mushrooms en Papillote (page 102), which she made again for her dad's birthday.

Probably more than anything else, though, Shorey likes to make desserts. We made a special raspberry cake (Shorey's Raspberry Cake, page 146) that she has baked for her mother's birthday, and a Strawberry Shortcake (page 142). Chocolate desserts are her favorite, so she particularly liked making Chocolate, Nut, and Fruit Treats (page 158).

Most of all, I wanted us to spend time together. I also wanted to teach her respect for ingredients. In the videos that we filmed with these recipes, she has a natural way of handling food, which helps her recover, even when she makes a mistake. Her innate elegance and poise are evident on film.

Shorey is thoughtful in giving me or her grandmother, father, or mother compliments, because she has a kind disposition and good manners, and she always smiles. We loved doing the show on table

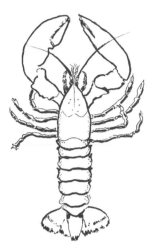

manners, where she corrected the way I sat at the table, my speaking with my mouth full, putting my elbows on the table, interrupting her when she spoke, slouching at the table, and the like. Shorey has very clear and precise opinions about life, cooking, school, and fun. She tells us bluntly what she likes and dislikes about cooking, what her favorite part of the meal is, and she remembers her first dish and the best restaurant she has eaten in. Of course, I think she is brilliant, but it is the prerogative of a grandfather to boast about his granddaughter.

Great meals are always the ones that are shared with family and friends. For me, that started many, many years ago in France and continued with Gloria and Claudine after I came to America. Now I'm sure that our family traditions, our kitchen legacy, will continue with Shorey.

"The first dish I remember my mom making is her spaghetti Bolognese; it is delicious. My dad's blueberry pie and his nachos are part of my earliest memories too."
—Shorey

Setting the Table

FOR A BASIC, SEMIFORMAL SETTING with only one set of silver-ware, the plates are put on nice placemats. The knife is placed to the right of the plate, cutting edge toward it, and the spoon (if needed) goes next to it. The fork or forks (dinner, salad) are placed to the left of the plate. Some people like to put the fork and spoon right side up, others upside down, which is less common. My wife always places a teaspoon crosswise above the main plate for dessert, although it can be

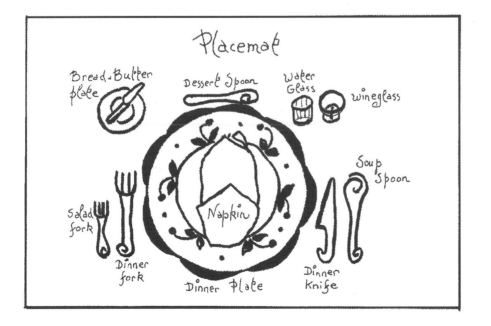

on the right. For more complex meals with more utensils (fish knife, sauce spoon), the knives, forks, and spoons are used starting with the one farthest out from the plate. The wineglass goes just above the tip of the knife and the water glass is to its left. Sometimes several glasses are used: champagne, white wine, red wine, cordial glasses.

Shorey and I write the guests' names on leaves (we use maple, oak, or ivy) and place them next to the plates or on the napkins.

There are many ways to fold napkins; here are five. Napkin 1 is just a square napkin folded in half. Napkin 2 is folded to create a 3-inch-wide strip and the strip is tied into a loose knot. For Napkin 3, two edges of a square napkin are folded underneath to create a point at the top and bottom. For Napkin 4, a square napkin is folded on itself halfway up and the left and right edges are folded underneath to create a small pocket in the center of the napkin, an opening for a piece of bread, a roll, or even a place card. For Napkin 5, the napkin is simply pulled through a napkin ring. The napkin goes to the left of the plate or on the plate itself (my preference).

To see how it's done, go to www.surlatable.com/jacquespepin.

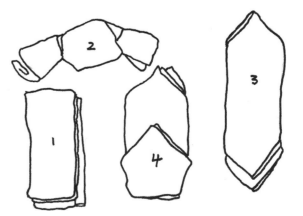

1 *Folding a napkin in style 3 (page 6)*

2

3

4

1 *Folding a napkin in style 4 (page 6)*

2

3

4

I've also taught Shorey the proper way to serve food from the left of the guests and beverages from the right. After the plates are used, they are picked up from the right, with the used silverware left on the plates.

Good Table Manners

SHOREY KNOWS HOW TO BEHAVE AT MEALTIME: Sit up straight, no elbows on the table. Do not start eating before the hostess does. Don't chew with your mouth open, do not make noise when chewing, and, especially, do not talk with your mouth full. Do not interrupt people. Bring the food up to your mouth, not vice versa. Shorey eats the European way, cutting the food with a knife held in her right hand, pushing it onto the fork, held in the left hand, and eating it from the fork. It is, however, perfectly correct to cut food with the knife in the right hand, place the knife back on the plate, pass the fork from the left to the right hand, and eat with the right hand. In that case, the left hand usually rests in the lap.

To see how it's done, go to www.surlatable.com/jacquespepin.

"I often set the table for dinner, but I usually forget the water glasses."
—Shorey

11

Hors d'Oeuvres

Hummus with Feta and Sunflower Seeds

One 15-ounce can chickpeas, or about 2 cups freshly cooked chickpeas, plus ¼ cup of the cooking liquid

4 garlic cloves

2 tablespoons fresh lemon juice

1 teaspoon hot chili sauce, such as Sriracha

½ teaspoon salt

½ cup extra-virgin olive oil

TOPPING

½ teaspoon Spanish smoked paprika

1 tablespoon extra-virgin olive oil

2 tablespoons crumbled feta cheese

2 tablespoons sunflower seeds

3 carrots, peeled and cut into 3- to 4-inch sticks (about 24)

3 or 4 celery stalks, trimmed and cut into 3- to 4-inch sticks (about 24)

12 scallions, cut into 3- to 4-inch lengths (about 24)

Hummus is always welcome with drinks at our house. Although it is classically made with chickpeas, I have made it with both cannellini and black beans. If you cook the chickpeas yourself, it will take about 2½ hours starting with cold water, but you can use canned. I garnish the hummus with crumbled feta cheese, sunflower seeds, a little olive oil, and Spanish paprika for a beautiful reddish top. Serve it with crackers, pita chips, or crudités, my choice here. Shorey loves raw vegetables, and she often eats hummus with radishes, cauliflower, mushrooms, and broccoli as well. This is a great dish to make for a kids' party, and it can be prepared ahead.

If using canned chickpeas, drain them and reserve ¼ cup of the liquid.

Process the garlic in a food processor for 10 seconds. Add the drained chickpeas, the reserved ¼ cup liquid, the lemon juice, chili sauce, and salt. Process for 15 seconds. Scrape down the sides of the processor bowl with a rubber spatula and process the mixture for another 15 seconds. Scrape down the sides of the bowl again and, with the processor running, add the olive oil. Continue processing for about 1 minute, until the hummus is very smooth and creamy.

Spread the hummus in a gratin dish; it should be about 1½ inches deep. Smooth the top and sprinkle on the paprika and then the oil, so the paprika combines with the oil. Scatter the feta cheese on top and sprinkle with the sunflower seeds. Arrange the vegetables around the edges and serve.

To see how it's done, go to www.surlatable.com/jacquespepin.

Radis au Beurre
(Radishes with Butter)

Radis au beurre instantly transports me to my childhood. The taste of small crunchy radishes slathered with butter and sprinkled with coarse salt is unequivocally part of a few essential tastes of my youth—along with bread and chocolate. The small radishes my mother grew or bought were the size of a baby carrot, red on top and white on the bottom. She'd split each radish open lengthwise three quarters of the way and open it like a flower, insert a piece of butter in the opening, and press the sides together to hold the butter in place. We'd dip the tip of each radish in coarse salt and consume them happily, with or without bread.

Today I use the big red crunchy radishes available at farmers' markets. I duplicate the treat of my youth by sandwiching some butter between two slices of radish and dipping that in salt. (Slice radishes into ¼-inch-thick slices, place about ¼ teaspoon butter on one radish slice, and press another slice on top. Dip one end of each "sandwich" in coarse salt and enjoy.) I also make a radish tartine, using coarse country bread that I cut into thin slices, slather with butter, load with thin slices of radish, and sprinkle with fleur de sel. These are one of my summer delights, and Shorey likes them as well.

Butter the slices of bread on one side and cut each slice across into 2 pieces. Arrange overlapping slices of radish on top, sprinkle with the salt, and serve.

SERVES 2

2½ tablespoons unsalted butter, softened

2 slices country bread (about 8 by 4 inches and ½ inch thick)

4 or 5 round red radishes, about 1½ inches in diameter, cut into 8 thin slices each

½ teaspoon fleur de sel or other coarse sea salt

Mini–Sweet Pepper Treats

MAKES 18 HORS D'OEUVRES

9 mini sweet bell peppers, halved
and seeded

Over the last few years, my market has been featuring small sweet bell peppers that are quite delicate—great for hors d'oeuvres or garnishes. Similar to Padrón peppers from Spain but sweeter, they can be cooked the same way as those peppers: sautéed in hot olive oil for 2 to 3 minutes, until browned all around and tender, then served with a sprinkling of coarse salt on top. They make a great accompaniment to grilled meat or poultry.

For this recipe, we halved the mini peppers lengthwise, removed the seeds, and garnished them with different fillings. Shorey likes cheese, shrimp, anchovies, and garlic, but you can use your inspiration to create new fillings, from scallops to olives to tomatoes to zucchini. Or just use one of our fillings for all of the peppers, increasing the amounts as needed.

The tiny peppers may be yellow or orange, but when they are cooked, they turn the same orange/yellow color. These make wonderful hors d'oeuvres for a cocktail party.

At serving time, heat the oven to 350 degrees.

For Filling #1, place 1 anchovy fillet in each of 6 pepper halves and cover with 2 garlic slivers and half a tomato. Drizzle ¼ teaspoon of the oil from the anchovies over each pepper.

For Filling #2, fill 6 pepper halves with the cheese and top with the jalapeños or Tabasco.

For Filling #3, mix all the ingredients together in a bowl and divide among the remaining 6 pepper halves.

Arrange all the pepper halves in a gratin dish in a single layer. Sprinkle the olive oil on top. Bake for 20 minutes, until the peppers are bubbling and cooked. Let cool to warm before serving.

"If I could have a meal with any group of people, I would invite Malala Yousafzai, Taylor Swift, Stephen Hawking, Albert Einstein (it's all relative!), and Barack Obama."
—Shorey

FILLING #1

6 anchovy fillets, with 1½ teaspoons of their oil

1 large garlic clove, sliced into 12 slivers with a vegetable peeler or a knife

3 small cherry tomatoes, halved

FILLING #2

2 ounces sharp cheddar cheese, cut into small dice or shredded

1 tablespoon coarsely chopped pickled jalapeño peppers, or a few drops of Tabasco sauce

FILLING #3

3 large shrimp, cooked, peeled, and coarsely chopped (about ½ cup)

1 tablespoon olive oil

2 teaspoons chopped fresh chives

¼ teaspoon salt

¼ teaspoon freshly ground black pepper

1 tablespoon olive oil

Deviled Eggs with Salmon (or Trout) Caviar

MAKES 12

6 large eggs, preferably organic

4 ounces Philadelphia cream cheese

2 tablespoons mayonnaise

1 teaspoon Dijon-style mustard

⅛ teaspoon salt

½ teaspoon freshly ground black pepper

2 tablespoons finely minced fresh chives

About 1 ounce salmon or trout caviar

Deviled eggs are festive, classic or new, fashionable, and delicious. Everybody loves them, and I wanted to make them with Shorey. The most important lesson in this recipe is proper cooking of the eggs. The details are important: from pricking the round end of the shells to relieve pressure and help prevent the eggs from cracking to cooling the cooked eggs in ice water to avoid the formation of a green tinge around the yolks and the smell of sulfur.

The stuffing mixture, made in seconds in a food processor, combines the egg yolks with cream cheese and a touch of mayonnaise and mustard. I garnish the eggs with salmon caviar, but you can use trout or sturgeon caviar instead. Or you could place a caper or an olive on top of each one, or a small piece of smoked salmon. Use your refrigerator and your imagination.

The deviled eggs can be made a few hours ahead.

Bring 6 cups water to a boil in a deep saucepan. Meanwhile, prick the rounded end of each egg with a pushpin or thumbtack.

Lower the eggs into the boiling water, and when the water comes back to a boil, reduce the heat so the water stays at a gentle boil. Cook the eggs for a total of 10 minutes.

Pour out the water and shake the pan to crack the eggshells all over. (This will help in the peeling of the eggs.) Immediately cover the eggs with cold water, add ice, and let cool for at least 15 minutes.

continued

When the eggs are cold, peel them under cool running water. Then cut a small sliver of white from both ends of each egg, so the stuffed half eggs can stand upright, and cut the eggs crosswise in half.

Carefully remove the yolks and place them in a food processor, along with the egg white trimmings, cream cheese, mayonnaise, mustard, salt, pepper, and 1 tablespoon of the chives. Process for a few seconds to combine the ingredients well.

The egg white halves can be stuffed using a spoon, but it is easier to do this with a pastry bag fitted with a star tip. Spoon the yolk mixture into the pastry bag and fill each egg white half with a rosette of the mixture.

Arrange the deviled eggs on a plate and top each with about ¼ teaspoon of the salmon caviar. Sprinkle the remaining chives on top and serve.

To see how it's done, go to www.surlatable.com/jacquespepin.

"I like to cook with Papi because I enjoy learning about his life and listening to his stories."
—Shorey

Hot Pâté in Puff Pastry

This classic French dish is quite complex to prepare the conventional way, with homemade puff pastry and a pâté mixture often involving game. But for this recipe, I use a sheet of store-bought puff pastry and make the pâté filling with a combination of sweet and hot Italian sausage. You can use bulk sausage meat or remove the casings from sausages. The pâté can be made ahead and frozen, which is a great plus, and then cooked when needed.

I showed Shorey two different ways to make this pâté. First I prepare two "logs" of pâté, wrapping the filling up in the dough to form a cylindrical shape. These are cut into pieces after they are baked and served as hors d'oeuvres. I then use the remaining dough and filling to make several individual pâtés, which can be served as a first course, along with a salad. Of course, you can instead make three logs for 30 hors d'oeuvres, or use all the dough and filling to make 9 individual pâtés.

Mix the meat, mushrooms, shallots, garlic, and wine together in a bowl. Divide the mixture into thirds. Beat the egg in a small bowl.

Sprinkle a little flour on your kitchen counter and, using a rolling pin, roll out the pastry sheet into a 12-inch square. Cut the sheet into 3 strips, each about 4 by 12 inches. Shape one third of the meat into a log down the center of one strip of dough. Wet the long edges of the dough with egg, bring the long edges of the dough together, pulling on the dough if you need to extend it, and press the edges together. Brush the log with egg and press on the edges with the tines of a fork to seal them well and create a design. Place the log on a baking sheet lined with nonstick aluminum foil. (Nonstick is important.) Repeat

MAKES 20 HORS D'OEUVRES,
PLUS 3 INDIVIDUAL PÂTÉS

8 ounces sweet Italian sausage, casings, if any, removed

4 ounces hot Italian sausage, casings, if any, removed

⅓ cup cleaned and coarsely chopped mushrooms (2 or 3 mushrooms)

3 tablespoons chopped shallot

1 teaspoon chopped garlic

¼ cup dry white wine

1 egg

2 or 3 tablespoons all-purpose flour

1 sheet frozen puff pastry (about 8 ounces, 9 inches by 9 inches)

with a second strip of dough and another third of the meat. *(The logs can be frozen until ready to bake; bake straight from the freezer.)*

FOR INDIVIDUAL PÂTÉS: Cut the third strip of dough into three 4-inch squares. Form the remaining meat into 3 balls and place a meatball in the center of each square of dough. Brush the surrounding dough with egg. Gently fold the four corners of the dough over so they meet in the center, then press down on the dough; each pâté will look like an open flower once it is baked. Brush with egg and place on a baking sheet lined with nonstick foil. *(The individual pâtés can also be frozen until ready to bake.)*

At baking time, preheat the oven to 425 degrees. Bake the logs and/or individual pâtés until well browned and cooked in the center, 35 to 40 minutes. Let the logs cool for a few minutes, then cut each one into 10 pieces.

Sushi Salmon Cubes

1 piece skinless salmon fillet or belly (about 6 ounces)

½ teaspoon salt

½ teaspoon freshly ground black pepper

½ teaspoon sugar

2 tablespoons chopped fresh chives

2 tablespoons chopped fresh parsley

2 tablespoons toasted sesame seeds

4 teaspoons toasted sesame oil

4 teaspoons peanut oil

At Shorey's age, I had never eaten raw fish, and when I first tried it, I did not like it. Things change, though, and now I do. Like many other children now, Shorey loves sushi, gravlax, smoked salmon, and the like.

This dish is prepared in a couple of minutes, and is ideal to pass around to your guests with aperitifs, drinks, or wine. The belly of the fish, which is fatter than the other parts of the fillet, is a choice piece for this recipe, but other fish can be substituted for salmon, with freshness being the most important factor. The curing and flavoring agents are simple: just salt, pepper, and sugar. The cubes of salmon should be no more than ¾ inch in size, so the salmon cures quickly. Alternatively, the salmon can be thinly sliced. Or find your own variation, one of the joys of cooking.

Cut the salmon into ¾-inch cubes. You should have about 30 cubes. Toss them with the salt, pepper, and sugar in a bowl. Refrigerate for 1 hour or up to 48 hours to cure.

When ready to serve, spread the salmon on a platter. Coat the cubes on all sides with the herbs and sesame seeds. Sprinkle the sesame and peanut oil on top. Insert a toothpick into each piece of salmon and pass the dish around for your guests to enjoy.

Soups and Salads

Creamy Tomato Soup

SERVES 8

2 tablespoons olive oil

2 cups diced (1-inch) onion

3 garlic cloves, crushed

1 tablespoon fresh thyme leaves,
   or 1 teaspoon dried thyme

1 tablespoon all-purpose flour

2½ cups water

2½ pounds very ripe tomatoes,
   cut into chunks

3 tablespoons tomato paste

2 teaspoons salt

1½ teaspoons sugar

1 teaspoon freshly ground black
   pepper

½ cup heavy cream

In summer, there is nothing like homemade tomato soup. With tomatoes at their peak flavor, best nutritional value, and cheapest price, I make hot, cold, chunky, smooth, and raw versions throughout the entire season.

Shorey's father, Rollie, is a great gardener, and Shorey loves the garden and its bounty. So we made this tomato soup together. For a lighter version, you can omit the flour and cream. The soup can be garnished with herbs from basil to chervil, tarragon, or chives, and it can be served hot, with croutons, if you like, or cold. Emulsifying the soup in a blender makes it smoother than if you use a food processor; for an even creamier result, you can finish the soup with a hand blender. Tomato soup with Grilled Cheese Sandwiches (page 57) makes the best possible lunch.

Heat the oil in a heavy saucepan. Add the onion and cook for 2 minutes over high heat. Stir in the garlic and thyme. Sprinkle the flour on top and mix well. Add the water and mix it in, then add the tomatoes, tomato paste, salt, sugar, and pepper and bring to a boil. Reduce the heat to low and cook, covered, for 15 minutes.

Let the soup cool for 15 to 30 minutes, then process it in batches in a stand blender for at least 30 seconds per batch. For an even creamier soup, transfer to a deep bowl and blend for 15 to 20 seconds with a hand blender. Stir in the cream. Serve hot or cold.

To see how it's done, go to www.surlatable.com/jacquespepin.

Soup with Vermicelle

This is a typical soup that my mother made when I was young. Claudine loves it as well, and it has become one of Shorey's favorites. My wife, Gloria, will often prepare this "fridge" soup to use up all the wilted vegetables and salad greens in the refrigerator—everything from a piece of onion or leek, half a zucchini, a carrot, scallions, parsley, celery, tomato, peas, or corn to leftover salad. I add some vermicelle (angel hair pasta or fine egg noodles—*vermicelli* in Italian) or alphabet noodles. When I was a kid, leftover bread was often a substitute for the pasta. I finish the soup with a little milk and grated Gruyère cheese, although both of these can be omitted.

Place the stock, salt, and leftover vegetables in a saucepan and bring to a boil. Stir well and boil for 5 minutes.

Add the pasta, bring to a boil, and boil gently for 5 minutes, or until the pasta is al dente.

Add the milk, if desired, stir, and serve sprinkled with the cheese, if you like.

To see how it's done, go to www.surlatable.com/jacquespepin.

SERVES 4

4 cups pork stock (from Spicy Ribs for Shorey, page 100) or store-bought chicken stock

½ teaspoon salt

4 cups coarsely chopped leftover vegetables and salad greens

1 cup vermicelle (fine egg noodles or angel hair pasta)

1 cup milk (optional)

½ cup grated Gruyère cheese (optional)

"The most fun thing about cooking is definitely eating."
—Shorey

Avocado, Tomato, and Mozzarella Salad

SERVES 2

1 ripe avocado (about 8 ounces)

1 tablespoon fresh lemon juice

2 scallions, thinly sliced (about ⅓ cup)

1 ripe tomato (about 8 ounces)

4 ounces mozzarella, cut into ½-inch dice (¾ cup)

2 tablespoons peanut or almond oil

¼ teaspoon salt

¼ teaspoon freshly ground black pepper

We especially like avocados and tomatoes at our house, and we always have avocados on hand to make a salad when they are ready—that is, ripe. I also use them in soup, as well as for guacamole. Gloria loves my garlic and chile pepper soup, made with long dried reddish-brown ancho or pasilla chile peppers, and served garnished with pieces of avocado.

With this recipe, I wanted to teach Shorey about avocados. We made a salad with the avocado flesh, tomato, mozzarella, and scallions and served it in the empty avocado shell. This makes a nice lunch for two.

Cut the avocado vertically in half all around the pit, twist the halves to separate them, and remove and discard the pit. Using a measuring teaspoon, scoop out pieces of avocado about the size of an olive; you should have about 15 scoops per half, or a good cup altogether. Reserve the avocado shells.

Place the avocado scoops in a bowl and toss with the lemon juice. Add the scallions.

Although the tomato can be used as is, my wife, Gloria, prefers it peeled. Using a sharp paring knife or vegetable peeler, remove the skin from the tomato, then cut the flesh into ½-inch dice. (You should have about 1¼ cups tomato.) Add to the bowl with the avocado, add the rest of the ingredients, and mix well.

At serving time, spoon about ½ cup of the salad onto each plate. Fill the avocado shells with the remainder of the salad and place one in the middle of the mixture on each plate, to secure the filled shell in place.

Beet and Apple Salad

Shorey particularly likes this sweet salad with red beets, apples, and pecans. I can buy vacuum-packed peeled precooked beets in my supermarket, and they are a real time-saver; if these aren't available where you live, boil or bake two or three beets until they are well cooked and tender. I always rinse my hands with water prior to handling red beets, which helps prevent staining, and I also line the cutting board with plastic wrap to prevent staining it. The apple adds sweetness and crunchiness, and the pecans lend texture and depth. The sour cream dressing is delicate and mild, and fresh dill finishes the salad nicely.

Place the beets in a colander and rinse them under cold water. Place them on a cutting board lined with plastic wrap and cut into ½- to ¾-inch dice. Put the diced beets in a bowl.

Peel and core the apple and cut it into ½-inch dice. Add to the bowl with the beets, then add the pecans, sour cream, vinegar, salt, and pepper. Mix well and set aside at room temperature until serving time (no more than 2 hours).

To serve, arrange 2 lettuce leaves on each of four plates. Top with the salad and garnish with the dill.

SERVES 4

1 package peeled cooked beets (about 8 ounces)

1 firm apple (about 8 ounces), such as Pippin, Red Delicious, or Granny Smith

⅓ cup pecan halves, broken into 2 or 3 pieces each

½ cup sour cream

1½ tablespoons red wine vinegar

½ teaspoon salt

½ teaspoon freshly ground black pepper

8 Boston lettuce leaves, preferably hydroponic

2 tablespoons chopped fresh dill sprigs

Egg, Tomato, and Anchovy Treats

Shorey is great at arranging ingredients in an artistic way on a plate. There is a lesson here in the cooking of the egg and in the presentation of the dish. It makes a nice lunch and is also a great starter for a summer dinner. Both Shorey and I like anchovies, but you don't have to use them if they are not to your taste.

FOR THE SAUCE: Mix all the ingredients together in a small bowl and set aside in the refrigerator.

Bring a small saucepan of water to a boil. Meanwhile, prick the rounded end of each egg with a pushpin or thumbtack. Lower the eggs into the boiling water, reduce the heat so the water barely boils, and cook the eggs for 10 minutes.

Pour off the water, shake the pan to crack the eggshells, and fill the pan with cold water. Add some ice to the pan to cool the eggs thoroughly.

After 15 minutes, or when the eggs are cold, shell them and cut each into quarters lengthwise. Cut each tomato lengthwise into quarters, then slit each quarter open. Split the anchovies lengthwise into halves.

Divide the sauce between two serving plates. Arrange 4 tomato quarters on each plate, placing them in the sauce so they meet in the center of the plate. Place an egg quarter in the opening of each tomato, with two of the egg quarters yolk side up and two yolk side down. Place an anchovy fillet half on each egg quarter and serve.

SERVES 2

SAUCE

3 tablespoons mayonnaise

2 tablespoons water

1 tablespoon sour cream

1 teaspoon rice vinegar

2 tablespoons chopped fresh parsley

⅛ teaspoon freshly ground black pepper

2 large eggs, preferably organic

2 plum tomatoes (about 3 ounces each)

4 anchovy fillets

Marinated Chinese Mushroom Salad

SERVES 4 TO 6

2 ounces (about 2 cups) dried tree ear mushrooms

DRESSING

1½ cups (5 ounces) thinly sliced mild onion, such as Vidalia or Maui

2 teaspoons chopped garlic

2 tablespoons dark soy sauce

2 tablespoons Chinese garlic chili sauce

1½ tablespoons Chinese black vinegar

1 tablespoon toasted sesame oil

1 teaspoon hot chili sauce, such as Sriracha

2 teaspoons sugar

¼ teaspoon salt

⅓ cup fresh cilantro leaves

Dried tree ear mushrooms are widely used in Chinese cooking, particularly in soups, stews, and salads. Most of these inexpensive mushrooms have little taste, but they do have a great chewy texture. They grow on tree trunks and are called by various names, including tree ear, wood ear, black ear, black fungus, Judas's ear, and cloud ear, which some people say is the larger variety. They have to be reconstituted in water, and the stems, if any, should be trimmed off, as they can be sandy. The mushrooms are then boiled for a few minutes before use in a dish. Tree ears don't get soft as they cook, retaining their crunchy texture. If possible, buy small ones, which have a better texture than the larger ones. (Dried Chinese seaweed is similar in color and can be prepared in the same manner.) Shorey loves Chinese food and is very fond of this salad.

Soak the mushrooms in 4 cups warm water in a saucepan for about 30 minutes, or until they rehydrate.

Lift the mushrooms from the water, remove and discard any tough stems, and cut them into 2- to 3-inch pieces. Return the mushrooms to the soaking water, bring to a boil, cover, and boil for 10 minutes. Set aside.

MEANWHILE, MAKE THE DRESSING: Mix all the ingredients except the cilantro together in a medium bowl.

Drain the mushrooms and add them, still warm, to the dressing. Toss well and let marinate for a few hours, tossing occasionally, until ready to serve.

Serve the salad with the cilantro sprinkled on top.

Potato Salad with Mayogrette Dressing

The word *mayogrette* is a contraction of "mayonnaise" and "vinaigrette," and this combination, which Shorey and I invented, is a smooth, silky dressing that can be used on all kinds of salads, from green salad to potato to lentil to beans to beet and other vegetable salads.

Put the potatoes in a medium saucepan, cover with water, add a pinch of salt, and bring to a boil. Reduce the heat and boil gently for about 35 minutes, until the potatoes are tender. Make sure to keep the potatoes covered with water, adding additional water if necessary. Drain.

When the potatoes are cool enough to handle, peel them and cut them into 1-inch cubes. (You should have about 3 cups.) Put them in a bowl and toss with the scallions, parsley, ¼ teaspoon salt, the pepper, and the dressing. The salad is best served slightly tepid or at room temperature.

SERVES 4

1 pound medium Yukon Gold potatoes (about 4 potatoes)

Salt

2 scallions, minced (about ¼ cup)

1 tablespoon chopped fresh parsley

¼ teaspoon freshly ground pepper

6 tablespoons Mayogrette Dressing (recipe follows)

Mayogrette Dressing

Put the mayonnaise, mustard, water, vinegar, salt, and pepper in a jar. Add half the oil, cover tightly with the lid, and shake well to emulsify the ingredients. Add the rest of the oil, replace the lid, and shake again until the mixture is smooth and creamy. The dressing can be refrigerated for several weeks.

To see how it's done, go to www.surlatable.com/jacquespepin.

MAKES ABOUT 1 CUP

2 tablespoons mayonnaise

2 tablespoons Dijon-style mustard

2 tablespoons water

1 tablespoon cider vinegar

¼ teaspoon salt

½ teaspoon freshly ground black pepper

½ cup extra-virgin olive oil

Tomato Salad

This is the simplest possible recipe, but I feel it is important for Shorey to realize that such a recipe can also be very sophisticated. The ripeness, temperature, and quality of the tomatoes, whether fresh out of the garden or organic heirlooms from the market, are important to the success of the dish. My wife, Gloria, likes her tomatoes peeled for this salad, and I prefer mine unpeeled. So, in this recipe, one tomato is peeled for Shorey's grandmother, the other one is not. Another consideration is how to slice the tomato properly and what else to add: coarse salt (I like fleur de sel), freshly ground black pepper, and the best olive oil. No vinegar or other acid is needed, because there is enough natural acid in the tomato flesh. The tomatoes are topped with mild onion slices and chives, or other herbs such as basil or parsley.

Remove the stems and cores from the tomatoes. Using a knife or vegetable peeler, gently remove the skin from one of the tomatoes. Alternatively, drop the tomato in boiling water for 10 seconds to loosen the skin, then peel it, or hold the tomato over the flame of a gas burner to loosen the skin enough so you can peel it off.

Place the tomatoes on their sides and cut each into 4 slices about ⅜ inch thick. Arrange the tomato slices on a plate and sprinkle with the salt and pepper. Separate the onion into rings and arrange on top of the tomato slices. Sprinkle with the olive oil and the chives.

NOTE: This salad can be prepared just a few minutes or up to 1 hour ahead. It should be served at room temperature.

SERVES 2

2 ripe tomatoes (6 to 7 ounces each)

½ teaspoon fleur de sel or other coarse sea salt

½ teaspoon freshly ground black pepper

½ cup thinly sliced sweet onion, such as Vidalia or Maui

2½ tablespoons extra-virgin olive oil

1 tablespoon chopped fresh chives

Salad Vinaigrette

With this recipe, I showed Shorey how to make a standard vinaigrette in a jar, so it can be ready as needed to dress a salad. The vinaigrette is not emulsified, so it has to be shaken each time it is used. For a variation, substitute 1 tablespoon toasted sesame oil or walnut oil for 1 tablespoon of the other oil.

The salad greens should be washed and dried thoroughly, cool but not ice-cold, and dressed with the vinaigrette no more than 30 minutes before serving. I like a mix of baby lettuce, preferably organic. When tossed with the vinaigrette, the greens will be glossy and shiny, without clumps of dressing attached to the leaves.

Put the vinegar, mustard, salt, and pepper in a jar and shake well. Add the oil and shake again, so the vinaigrette is thoroughly mixed. It will not be emulsified, and the oil will separate out. Keep the dressing refrigerated until ready to use, and shake well before using.

TO SERVE 1: Mix 2 loose cups salad greens with 1 tablespoon of vinaigrette.

TO SERVE 4: Mix 8 loose cups salad greens with 4 tablespoons of vinaigrette.

To see how it's done, go to www.surlatable.com/jacquespepin.

MAKES 1 CUP

3 tablespoons red wine vinegar

2 tablespoons Dijon-style mustard

¼ teaspoon salt

½ teaspoon freshly ground black pepper

⅔ cup peanut, grapeseed, safflower, or extra-virgin olive oil

Chicken Grits Soup and Chicken Salad (pages 44—45)

Chicken Grits Soup and Chicken Salad

SERVES 2

STOCK

4 cups water

2 teaspoons chicken base, preferably organic

½ cup peeled and diced (½-inch) carrot

½ cup cleaned and diced (½-inch) leek

½ cup diced (½-inch) onion

½ cup cleaned and diced (½-inch) mushrooms

2 skinless, boneless chicken breasts (5 to 6 ounces each)

DRESSING

2 tablespoons finely chopped onion

2 tablespoons finely chopped fresh parsley

½ teaspoon finely chopped garlic

1½ tablespoons mayonnaise

1½ tablespoons extra-virgin olive oil

1½ teaspoons Dijon-style mustard

For this salad, I use boneless, skinless chicken breasts. I usually buy organic chicken breasts. First I make a stock with vegetables and a bit of organic chicken base, which just needs to boil for 5 to 6 minutes. Then I cook the chicken briefly in the stock, cover the pot, and allow the chicken to poach in the hot liquid off the heat for 20 minutes. This method produces tender, juicy meat. Once it is cool, the meat is shredded by hand, tossed with a mustardy dressing, and served at room temperature. Shorey and I have great fun with the presentation of this dish. We use radishes, romaine lettuce, tomato, hard-cooked eggs, and chives to decorate the salad and make it look like a chicken on the plate.

Kids love to make these decorations. You can also use olives, bell pepper strips, basil leaves, and other ingredients to create your own design. Make sure that all the decorative elements are good with the salad.

Then, for the soup, grits (or polenta, basically the same thing) are added to the stock and boiled for a couple of minutes to create a hearty, delicious dish that can be served on its own or with grated Parmesan or Gruyère on top. The soup can also be made using just the stock base and grits, without the chicken breasts.

FOR THE STOCK: Place all the stock ingredients in a pot and bring to a boil. Boil gently for about 6 minutes. *(This can be done ahead.)*

WHEN READY TO MAKE THE SALAD: Add the chicken breasts to the stock and bring to a boil (this will take about 4 minutes). Boil gently for about 45 seconds, then cover the pot and remove it from the heat. Let the chicken poach gently in the hot stock for 20 minutes.

Remove the breasts from the stock and, when they are cool enough to handle, tear into pieces following the grain of the meat. Reserve the stock for the soup.

FOR THE DRESSING: Mix all the ingredients together.

FOR THE SALAD: Toss the chicken well with the dressing. The salad can be served as is or spooned onto lettuce leaves. Or, for a more elegant presentation, use the optional ingredients to make a decorative "chicken": A slice from the center of the hard-cooked egg will be the head of the chicken. Fashion a beak, comb, and feet from outside slices of radish. Arrange the chicken salad on a plate to create the body of the bird and use a small lettuce leaf to make the tail. Cut one of the outside tomato slices so it resembles feathers and use the other as the tail of the bird. Arrange a few chives on top to simulate more feathers and use lettuce ribs and pecans for the feet.

FOR THE SOUP: Bring the stock to a boil, add the grits or polenta, and bring back to a boil. Boil for about 3 minutes, until the grits are cooked. Serve with grated Parmesan or Gruyère cheese or, if you prefer, as is.

To see how it's done, go to www.surlatable.com/jacquespepin.

1 tablespoon red wine vinegar

¼ teaspoon Tabasco sauce

½ teaspoon salt

Lettuce leaves, for serving (optional)

OPTIONAL (FOR PRESENTATION)

1 hard-cooked egg, sliced with an egg slicer

1 or 2 large radishes

Some small romaine lettuce leaves

A few fresh chives

SOUP

⅓ cup grits or polenta, preferably organic stone-ground

Grated Parmesan or Gruyère, for serving (optional)

Eggs, Sandwiches, Pizza, and Breads

Fried Eggs Sunny-Side Up with Cheese and Herbs

SERVES 2

2 teaspoons unsalted butter

2 large eggs, preferably organic

Salt

Freshly ground black pepper (optional)

1 teaspoon grated Parmesan cheese

1 teaspoon chopped fresh chives

1½ teaspoons water

Toast, for serving (optional)

Crisp bacon (see opposite), for serving (optional)

A plate of sunny-side up fried eggs is perfect for breakfast or lunch, but the eggs are often fried until the edges of the whites get too brown, curl up, and are tough. My taste is for tender egg whites with no curled edges and yolks that are slightly runny and glazed on top. To cook the eggs properly, the butter should be foaming but not too hot. The heat should be low to medium, and the pan covered. When the eggs are half-cooked, I add a bit of water to the pan. The water creates steam in the covered skillet as they cook, and the tops of the yolks glaze beautifully. These are sometimes called "mirror eggs" because of their shiny tops.

Heat the butter in a 6-inch nonstick skillet (with a lid) until it is just melted, taking care not to let it get too hot. Crack the eggs into the skillet, season with a dash each of salt and pepper, if you like, cover, and cook over low heat for about 1½ minutes. Sprinkle the eggs with the cheese and chives, add the water, cover, and cook for another minute, or until the tops of the yolks are glazed.

Transfer to a serving plate. Serve right away with toast and bacon, if desired. I like to cut the crust off the toast and slice it into "soldiers"—about ¾-inch-wide batons.

To see how it's done, go to www.surlatable.com/jacquespepin.

Crisp Bacon

Years ago, my wife showed me how to cook bacon in a microwave oven. It is still the best method for me, and Shorey enjoys doing it too. Depending on the thickness of the bacon, the power of your microwave oven, and your taste preferences (crisp or very crisp bacon), the cooking time varies. I cook my bacon for 4 minutes at full power, and if that is not enough, I cook it in 30-second increments until it is done to my taste (usually in 3½ to 4 minutes). It is great in BLTs and other sandwiches, with fried eggs, or crumbled in a salad.

Don't forget to cover the bacon with paper towels to prevent it from splattering all over the microwave.

Line a large plate with paper towels and arrange the bacon slices on top. The slices should touch but not overlap. Place a piece of paper towel over the bacon, so it rests on top. Place in the microwave and cook at full power for 3 minutes, then check the bacon. Microwave for another 30 seconds if you like it crisper, and then for another 20 to 30 seconds, if needed. Let cool for a few minutes and enjoy.

**MAKES 6 SLICES
(ABOUT 4 OUNCES)**

6 slices bacon (preferably lean),
about 4 ounces

Cottage Cheese Pancakes with Blueberries

MAKES 8 PANCAKES

BATTER

2 large eggs, preferably organic

¼ cup sour cream

½ teaspoon pure vanilla extract

1 tablespoon sugar

⅛ teaspoon salt

½ cup all-purpose flour

½ cup cottage cheese

2 tablespoons unsalted butter

2 tablespoons peanut, grapeseed, or safflower oil

GARNISH

¼ cup apricot preserves

1 cup blueberries

This is one of Gloria's recipes that she often makes for Shorey's breakfast when she stays at our house. Shorey always eats fruit for breakfast, and she is very fond of blueberries, so we mix the berries with apricot preserves to serve with the pancakes. (I heat the preserves in a microwave oven for a few seconds, so they liquefy and combine well with the blueberries.) You can use honey or sour cream instead or substitute other berries for the blueberries.

I mix the ingredients in a small food processor and add the cottage cheese at the end, pulsing it for only a few seconds so it keeps a bit of its texture.

Put the eggs, sour cream, vanilla, sugar, salt, and flour in a small food processor in this order and process for about 15 seconds, until smooth. Add the cottage cheese and process for a few seconds, just enough to mix it in.

Heat 1 tablespoon each of the butter and oil in a 10- to 12-inch nonstick skillet. Add about 3 tablespoons of batter for each pancake, making 4 pancakes at a time, and cook for about 3 minutes on the first side. Flip and cook for 1½ to 2 minutes on the other side. Transfer the pancakes to a plate and repeat, heating the remaining butter and oil and making a second batch of pancakes with the rest of the batter.

Meanwhile, heat the apricot preserves in a microwave oven for about 30 seconds to liquefy them, then mix with the blueberries.

Serve the warm pancakes with the blueberries.

To see how it's done, go to www.surlatable.com/jacquespepin.

Easy Cheese Soufflé/Flan

This is not really a soufflé or a flan, but a mixture of the two; it could be called a *"soufflan."* For a soufflé, the eggs are separated and the whites are beaten to give volume to the soufflé. Here the eggs are mixed with cream cheese and cottage cheese and cooked in a gratin dish. The mixture puffs up as it cooks, but not as much as a soufflé would. This is easier to make than a soufflé, though it takes a few minutes longer to cook.

Shorey loves the taste, texture, and look of this dish, and I wanted to show her how to make it for her family. Serve it puffy and hot right from the oven, or allow it to deflate and serve lukewarm with a vinaigrette-dressed lettuce salad.

Heat the oven to 375 degrees.

Place the cottage cheese, cream cheese, eggs, salt, and pepper in a food processor and process for 10 to 15 seconds. Add the chives and process again.

Rub a 4- to 5-cup gratin dish with the olive oil and fill with the egg mixture. Place the gratin dish on a baking sheet and bake for 40 to 45 minutes, or until the soufflé/flan is just set. Serve immediately, or allow to deflate and serve lukewarm.

SERVES 4

One 16-ounce container cottage cheese

One 8-ounce container whipped cream cheese

4 large eggs, preferably organic

¼ teaspoon salt

½ teaspoon freshly ground black pepper

3 tablespoons minced fresh chives

1 teaspoon olive oil

"When we cook together, my dad and I usually make breakfast."
—Shorey

Cucumber-Dill Sandwiches

The elegant, classic British cucumber sandwich involves a lot of techniques for me to show Shorey. First I demonstrated how to cut the cucumber into very thin slices with a vegetable peeler. Then I made real Melba toast by toasting thin white bread slices (I like Pepperidge Farm Original White Bread) and then slicing each warm toasted slice horizontally to separate it into two crispy squares. (These super-thin toasts were created by Chef Auguste Escoffier in the late 1800s for Nellie Melba, an opera singer who loved her toast very thin.) Finally, I coated the edges of the sandwiches with chopped dill. I described a traditional British afternoon tea for Shorey, including an assortment of possible tea varieties; different finger sandwiches, like cucumber, watercress, and smoked salmon; and the classic scones, clotted cream, and fruit preserves. I also talked about *quatre heure,* 4 o'clock teatime in France.

Cut the cucumber in half crosswise and save one half for another dish. Using a vegetable peeler, peel the cucumber half and, still using the peeler, cut thin lengthwise slices from one side of the cucumber until you see the seeds; then turn the cucumber and continue cutting long slices until only the seedy center remains; discard the seeds. Place the cucumber slices in a bowl, toss with the salt, and set aside for 10 minutes.

Meanwhile, spread the chopped dill on a plate.

Toast the bread slices in a toaster until nicely browned. Trim off the crusts to create square slices. Place the toasts flat on a board and, using a small thin knife, cut through the middle of the bread slices

MAKES 2 SANDWICHES

1 cucumber (about 8 ounces)

⅛ teaspoon salt

2 tablespoons chopped fresh dill

2 slices thin white sandwich bread (about 4 inches square)

¼ cup mayonnaise

⅛ teaspoon freshly ground black pepper

to separate them each into 2 thin slices, or Melba toasts. Rotating the bread as you slice through it makes this easier.

Coat the soft side of each toast with some of the mayonnaise. Place the cucumber slices on paper towels to absorb most of the liquid they have released, then divide them between 2 of the toasts and sprinkle with the pepper. Place the remaining 2 toasts mayonnaise side down over the cucumbers. Holding one sandwich in your hand, coat the edges thinly with mayonnaise and press the edges into the chopped dill on the plate so it sticks to them. Repeat with the other sandwich.

Cut the sandwiches in half diagonally and serve.

To see how it's done, go to www.surlatable.com/jacquespepin.

Croque Shorey

2 large slices multigrain bread
(4 ounces; about 7 by 4 inches)

4 slices sharp white cheddar
cheese (about 3 ounces)

About 3 ounces sliced cooked
turkey

2 lightly packed cups (2 ounces)
baby spinach, microwaved for
1 minute

1 small ripe tomato (about
4 ounces), cut into 4 or 5 slices

1 tablespoon peanut or olive oil

A Croque Monsieur is the classic French grilled ham and cheese sandwich, and the Croque Madame is a similar sandwich made with chicken rather than ham. This croque is made with Shorey's favorite ingredients: sharp white cheddar cheese, roast turkey, spinach, and tomatoes, on hearty multigrain bread. The recipe makes a very large, flavorful sandwich. It consists of seven layers—bread, cheese, turkey, spinach, tomato slices, cheese, and then bread. It can also be served unbaked. The sandwich is very good served with a green salad.

It can be assembled way ahead and then baked for about 15 minutes in a 400-degree oven when ready to serve. It takes that amount of time to soften the tomato, melt the cheese, and brown the bread properly. Although the spinach could be added raw, the amount is voluminous (about 2 cups) and would be hard to secure between the bread slices, so I microwave it for 1 minute to wilt it and make it easy to fit into the sandwich.

Heat the oven to 400 degrees.

Lay the bread slices on the counter and cover one of them with 2 slices of the cheese. Top with the sliced turkey and then the blanched spinach. Cover with the tomato slices, then add the remaining 2 slices cheese and, finally, the second slice of bread.

Pour the oil onto an aluminum foil–lined baking sheet and spread it evenly to about the dimensions of the sandwich. Press the sandwich into it, then turn the sandwich over so it is oiled on both sides. Bake for 15 minutes, until the bread is brown, the tomatoes are soft, the cheese is melted, and the inside of the sandwich is warm. Remove from the oven, cut in half, and serve right away.

To see how it's done, go to www.surlatable.com/jacquespepin.

Grilled Cheese Sandwiches

These sandwiches should really be called baked cheese sandwiches, as I make them in the oven. They are a classic accompaniment to Tomato Soup (page 30) for a great lunch. I like to use regular white sandwich bread and sharp cheddar cheese slices that are about the same size as the bread. I add a bit of hot red salsa to give a tang to the sandwiches, but it can be omitted, if you prefer.

Heat the oven to 400 degrees.

Line a baking sheet with aluminum foil. Pour the oil on top and spread it over the foil with your fingers.

Place 2 slices of the cheese on one slice of bread. Spread 1 tablespoon of the hot salsa on top, if desired, and cover with another slice of bread. Repeat with the remaining bread, cheese, and salsa to make a second sandwich.

Press one side of each sandwich into the oil on the baking sheet, then turn over so both sides of the sandwiches are coated with oil. Bake for 13 to 15 minutes, until the sandwiches are nicely browned. Let cool for a few minutes before cutting in half and serving.

MAKES 2 SANDWICHES

1 tablespoon grapeseed or canola oil

4 slices sharp cheddar cheese (about 3½ inches square)

4 slices white sandwich bread (3½ to 4 inches square)

2 tablespoons hot red salsa (optional)

Rice Paper Vegetable Rolls

SERVES 6

12 rice paper spring roll wrappers
(8 to 9 inches in diameter)

1 carrot, peeled and shredded
(about 1 cup)

6 thin scallions, cut into pieces
about 1 inch long

1 avocado (about 8 ounces),
halved, pitted, peeled, and cut
into 12 wedges

1 tablespoon fresh lemon juice

2 radishes, thinly sliced with a
vegetable peeler or a sharp
knife

12 fresh basil leaves

12 oil-cured black olives, pitted
and cut into ½-inch pieces

SAUCE

2 tablespoons dark soy sauce

1 tablespoon hoisin sauce

1 tablespoon rice vinegar

1 tablespoon maple syrup

1 teaspoon hot chili sauce, such
as Sriracha

Shorey loves raw vegetables, so I decided to make these rice paper rolls with her. Here, I fill the rolls with fresh vegetables, but feel free to use whatever is at hand: shrimp, salad, dried tomatoes, leftover meat or fish. I make a sauce with soy, hoisin, and sesame oil, but mayonnaise with hot sauce or sour cream is appropriate as well. I assemble no more than three rolls at a time, because the wrappers tend to dry out on the work surface. I also dampen the board I roll them on, so they stay pliable. Although one wrapper per roll is the conventional choice, I use two rice papers for each roll because I like the chewiness and texture and these tend to be sturdier; you can use just one per roll if you prefer. All they need is to be moistened on both sides with water; after about 20 seconds, they become soft and pliable.

Rice paper spring roll wrappers are available at Asian markets or on the internet. The rolls can be prepared a couple of hours ahead. Cover so they don't dry out, and refrigerate.

Run 3 of the rice papers under cold water to moisten them on both sides and place them on a wet cutting board. After 20 or 30 seconds, they will soften and become pliable. Place some shredded carrot and a few pieces of scallion in the center of each wrapper; leave at least 1 inch of rice paper visible on both sides of the vegetables. Mix the avocado slices with the lemon juice and place 2 wedges on each wrapper. Add a few slices of radish, 2 basil leaves, and some pieces of olive.

Fold about one third of the top part of the wrapper over the vegetables, then bring the sides of the wrapper over the vegetables and roll up to create a secure roll. Repeat with another 3 wrappers to make a total of 6 rolls. Moisten the remaining 6 wrappers and wrap a second rice paper wrapper around each roll.

FOR THE SAUCE: Mix all the ingredients together in a small bowl. Serve the rolls whole or in halves, with the dipping sauce.

To see how it's done, go to www.surlatable.com/jacquespepin.

Tortilla Pizzas

I have enjoyed pizza in China, Mexico, Turkey, Russia, France, Spain, and, of course, Italy—I believe it is the most popular dish in the world. It transcends nationalities, cultures, cuisines, and traditions.

Instead of pizza dough, Shorey and I use tortillas.

MAKES TWO 8-INCH PIZZAS; SERVES 2

3 tablespoons extra-virgin olive oil

2 large (8- to 9-inch) flour tortillas

2 cups loosely packed (about 2 ounces) baby spinach

2 ripe tomatoes (about 5 ounces each), cut into 6 slices each

½ teaspoon salt

½ teaspoon freshly ground black pepper

1½ cups grated Gruyère, Emmenthaler, or Jarlsberg cheese

2 tablespoons grated Parmesan cheese

Heat the oven to 400 degrees.

Line a baking sheet with aluminum foil. Pour 1 tablespoon of the olive oil on top and spread it over the foil. Press the 2 tortillas into the oil, then turn them over so they are coated with oil on both sides. Press and pack 1 cup of the spinach onto each tortilla. Arrange 6 slices of tomato on top of the spinach on each one; the tomato slices will hold the spinach in place. Sprinkle the tomatoes with the salt and pepper, then add the Gruyère and Parmesan cheeses. Sprinkle on the remaining 2 tablespoons olive oil.

Place in the oven and bake for 15 minutes, or until nicely browned.

"The hardest thing to deal with in the kitchen, for me, is usually the stove."
—Shorey

English Muffin Pizzas

Gloria and Shorey make several variations on this recipe, topping the muffins with olives, tomatoes, anchovy fillets, mushrooms, and the like. The muffin halves are toasted until nicely browned and hard on top; this is important, because garlic is then rubbed over the hard brown surface, abrading it and giving the bread a wonderful taste and smell. If the surface of the muffins is still soft, the technique won't work. Then the muffins are topped with ham and cheese, and a little oil and pepper, and placed under a hot broiler until the cheese is melted and bubbling.

Place an oven rack 7 or 8 inches below the broiler and turn the broiler on.

Split the muffins into halves with your hands, a fork, or a knife. Place the halves in a toaster and toast until nicely browned. Rub the garlic firmly over the surface of the toasted muffin halves. (You should use most of the garlic.)

Arrange the muffin halves on a baking sheet lined with aluminum foil. Cover with the ham slices and then the cheese. Sprinkle with the oil and pepper. Place the baking sheet under the hot broiler and cook for 4 to 5 minutes, until the cheese is melted and bubbling.

Garnish the pizzas with the parsley and serve immediately.

MAKES 4 SMALL MUFFIN PIZZAS; SERVES 2

2 English muffins

1 large garlic clove, peeled

4 slices boiled ham (about 2 ounces)

4 slices sharp cheddar cheese (about 2 ounces)

2 teaspoons olive oil

⅛ teaspoon freshly ground black pepper

1 teaspoon chopped fresh parsley

Little Rolls and Breadsticks

MAKES 6 ROLLS
AND 6 BREADSTICKS

4 teaspoons olive oil

1½ pounds store-bought pizza dough

FOR THE ROLLS

½ teaspoon Spanish smoked (or regular) paprika

½ teaspoon herbes de Provence or Italian seasoning

1 teaspoon coarse salt, or to taste

FOR THE STICKS

¼ teaspoon garlic powder

¼ teaspoon freshly ground black pepper

1 tablespoon grated Parmesan cheese

Freshly baked bread with butter is about as good as it gets. I have made many breads from scratch in my life, but I wanted to show Shorey an easy way to do it using pizza dough, which is readily available in supermarkets. The dough can be shaped into a long, flat bread or baguette-style bread or, as in this recipe, into small individual rolls and breadsticks, each weighing about 2 ounces.

We used one topping for the rolls and another for the sticks. We flavored the rolls with smoked paprika, herbes de Provence (or Italian seasoning), and coarse salt, while we sprinkled the sticks with garlic powder, black pepper, and grated Parmesan cheese. You can create your own toppings or just cook the rolls and sticks plain. These are made in minutes, then allowed to rise for 30 minutes before baking.

Line a jelly-roll pan (12 by 17 inches) with aluminum foil. Pour the olive oil onto the foil-lined sheet and spread it over the foil.

Using a sharp knife, cut the dough in half. Cut one of the halves into 6 pieces for the rolls. Flatten the other half of the dough into a square with your fingers and cut it into 6 strips.

FOR THE ROLLS: Shape the pieces of dough by pressing on them with your hands in a circular motion. Press the formed rolls into the oil on the foil-lined sheet, then flip them over so they are oiled on both sides. Arrange the rolls at least 1 inch apart on one half of the pan. Sprinkle with the paprika, herbes de Provence (or Italian seasoning), and coarse salt.

FOR THE BREADSTICKS: Pull on the strips of dough to make sticks about the width of the pan and roll them on the pan so they are coated with the oil, then arrange them about 1 inch apart. Sprinkle the sticks with the garlic powder, pepper, and Parmesan.

Cover the pan with an upside-down jelly-roll pan and let the dough proof for about 30 minutes at room temperature. Meanwhile, heat the oven to 425 degrees.

When the dough is ready, remove the top pan and place the baking pan in the oven. Cook the breadsticks for 20 to 25 minutes and the rolls for 25 to 30 minutes. Let cool and enjoy.

A Lesson on Leftover Bread

TOASTED BAGUETTE SLICES
AND CROUTONS (OR BREAD
CRUMBS)

1 leftover baguette or piece of
  baguette (about 6 ounces),
  cut into 15 slices (about ⅜ inch
  thick)

2 tablespoons olive oil

WHOLE LOAF

1 baguette or country loaf

I never throw bread away. My father would turn over in his grave! Bread is the staff of life and should be respected as such. Leftover bread, whether a country loaf, baguette, or sliced bread, does get stale after a couple of days, but there are still many ways to use it. It can be cubed for croutons and added to salads or turned into crumbs and sprinkled on top of a gratin or sautéed vegetables, or on fish, meat, or poultry, as well as over soups. Stale slices of bread soaked in a mixture of milk and eggs, then sautéed in butter and sprinkled with sugar make excellent French toast.

I wanted Shorey to understand how important bread is and how to use it when it is stale. The bread I had on hand was a baguette that was a couple of days old and a bit dry. Timing will change depending on the staleness of the bread and how thick the loaf or slices are. Dampening the bread reintroduces moisture and makes it very crispy. When preparing wet bread slices in a toaster, you may have to toast the bread twice so the slices brown and get crusty. For croutons, slices of bread can be coated with oil and browned in the oven. For use in soups or salads, crush them with the back of a skillet into coarse crumbs. A whole reconstituted baguette will be crisp outside and moist inside for just a few hours, so it should consumed fairly quickly.

FOR TOASTED BAGUETTE SLICES: Run 5 slices of the baguette briefly under water. They should be barely wet on the outside, not soaked through. Place the slices in a toaster for 4 to 5 minutes, until nicely browned and crusty; you may have to toast them twice.

FOR CROUTONS OR BREAD CRUMBS: Heat the oven to 400 degrees.

Spread the oil on a baking sheet lined with aluminum foil. Press the remaining 10 baguette slices into the oil, turning to coat on both sides. Bake for 10 to 12 minutes, until well browned and crusty. Leave whole for croutons, or coarsely crush into crumbs.

FOR WHOLE LOAF: Heat the oven to 400 degrees.

Run the bread under running water for a few seconds to wet the outside. Place directly on the oven rack and heat until hard and crusty on top and soft inside, about 15 minutes for a baguette and a few minutes longer for a large country loaf. Slice and eat within a few hours.

To see how it's done, go to www.surlatable.com/jacquespepin.

"My favorite part of the meal is almost always dessert, but when it's not, it's the bread!"
—Shorey

Fish and Shellfish

Mushroom and Scallop Toasts

SERVES 4 AS A MAIN COURSE; 8 AS A FIRST COURSE

3 tablespoons olive oil

About 10 ounces firm baby bella mushrooms, cleaned and sliced (you can use an egg slicer; about 3 cups)

1 pound bay scallops or large sea scallops, cut into 1-inch pieces if using sea scallops

1 tablespoon chopped garlic (about 3 cloves)

½ cup chopped fresh parsley

¾ teaspoon salt

¾ teaspoon freshly ground black pepper

2 tablespoons unsalted butter

4 slices bread (6 to 7 ounces), preferably 7-grain, toasted, and cut in half if serving as a first course

For this recipe, I showed Shorey how to slice mushrooms using an egg slicer, and she got a kick out of doing it. Cooking should be sharing and fun, and that is how you develop the palate of a child.

I also wanted to teach Shorey quick dishes that can be served either as a main course or as a first course for a formal dinner. This dish fits the bill. I use scallops, but shrimp or salmon can be substituted with excellent results. The mushrooms and scallops can also be served without the bread.

Heat the olive oil in a large skillet. Add the sliced mushrooms and sauté over high heat for about 4 minutes. Add the scallops, garlic, parsley, salt, pepper, and butter and sauté for about 3 minutes, until the scallops are just barely cooked.

Arrange a bread slice on each of four plates. Divide the scallop and mushroom mixture among the bread and serve immediately.

"Cooking with my grandmother does not happen very often—we usually just go out together to our favorite Chinese restaurant so there is no cleanup."
—Shorey

Fish Fillets in Caper Sauce

Shorey told me that her mother often cooks pan-fried fish with a special sauce. So we duplicated this "secret sauce," which consists of capers, butter, lemon juice, and herbs, and served it with sautéed fish fillets. The recipe can be made with red snapper or cod, or you can substitute tilapia, black sea bass, or blackfish (tautog). The size and thickness of the fillets determine the cooking time. Freshest is best, of course, and the beauty of this type of recipe is that the fish takes only a few minutes to cook and then is served immediately. I have taught Shorey about endangered species of fish and how to find out which are threatened by consulting the Monterey Bay Aquarium website.

Dry the fish fillets with paper towels and sprinkle them with the salt and pepper. Spread the flour on a plate.

When ready to cook the fish, heat the oil in a large skillet until hot. Dip the fish in the flour to coat it on both sides. Place the fillets in the hot skillet and cook for about 1½ minutes on each side, so the fish is almost cooked through but slightly undercooked at the thicker end and still moist. Place the fillets on warm plates and sprinkle with the capers and lemon juice.

Add the butter to the drippings in the skillet and cook until the butter is lightly browned and very hot. Pour over the fillets, sprinkle with the parsley, and serve immediately.

SERVES 2

2 fish fillets, such as skinless red snapper or cod fillets (5 to 6 ounces each and about ⅓ inch thick at the thickest end)

½ teaspoon salt

½ teaspoon freshly ground black pepper

1½ tablespoons all-purpose flour

2 tablespoons sunflower or peanut oil

1½ tablespoons drained capers

1 tablespoon fresh lemon juice

2 tablespoons unsalted butter

1 tablespoon chopped fresh parsley

Lemon Sole with Butter and Lemon

SERVES 2

1½ tablespoons chopped fresh
  chives

¼ teaspoon salt

¼ teaspoon freshly ground black
  pepper

4 small fillets lemon sole (about
  2½ ounces each and ¼ to
  ⅜ inch thick)

1 tablespoon unsalted butter,
  softened

1 tablespoon fresh lemon juice

Lemon sole, which is very mild and delicate, can be broiled, sautéed, or poached, as in this recipe. Petrale sole, fluke, flounder, dab, or even Dover sole can be substituted for the lemon sole. Have the water near a boil, ready for the fish, but do not cook the fish until you are ready to serve. The fillets of sole Shorey and I use are very thin and even, and they cook in about 1½ minutes, not enough time for the water to come back to a boil.

The seasonings are simplicity itself: good butter, lemon juice, salt, pepper, and chives. The salt, pepper, and chives are mixed together to make them easy to sprinkle on the fish. Make sure that your dinner plates are hot and that you have paper towels to blot the water from the fish before placing the fillets on the plates.

Heat two dinner plates in a warm oven. Mix together the chives, salt, and pepper.

Bring 3 cups water to a boil in a 10- to 12-inch skillet. At serving time, slide the fish fillets into the water in one layer. Cook for about 1½ minutes (the water will not come back to a boil). Using a skimmer, lift out one fillet at a time and blot the top of the fish and the bottom of the skimmer with a paper towel, then place on a plate. Spread the soft butter on top of the fillets. Sprinkle with the lemon juice and the salt, pepper, and chive mixture. Serve immediately, with a sauce spoon or regular spoons.

To see how it's done, go to www.surlatable.com/jacquespepin.

Arctic Char with Tomato

In this recipe I cook a fillet of Arctic char on the skin side only in a nonstick pan. This recipe also works well with trout. The sauce is a raw tomato puree made in a blender and seasoned with salt, pepper, and olive oil. (It can also be used for pasta or as a summer soup, in which case it should be doubled.)

The pan should be preheated for about 1 minute so it is hot when the fish is placed in it.

Covering the fish during cooking creates steam, which allows the char to cook on top without being turned, and the hot pan delivers a crusty skin without the addition of oil or butter. This dish should be prepared at the last minute because the fish takes only a short time to cook.

FOR THE SAUCE: Place the tomato pieces in a blender and process for 15 to 20 seconds, until well pureed. Add the salt, pepper, and oil, and process for another 10 seconds. Set aside.

At cooking time, cut the fillet into 2 pieces. Rub the skin with the oil and sprinkle with the salt. Heat a 10-inch nonstick skillet over high heat for about 1 minute. Place the fish pieces skin side down in the skillet, cover, and cook over high heat for about 3 minutes. Remove the pan from the heat and continue cooking the char in the residual heat for about 1 minute.

Meanwhile, heat the sauce in the microwave until warm, about 1 minute. Divide it between two dinner plates, and place the fish skin side up in the sauce. Serve immediately.

To see how it's done, go to www.surlatable.com/jacquespepin.

SERVES 2

SAUCE

1 ripe tomato (about 6 ounces), stem and core removed, cut into 1-inch pieces

¼ teaspoon salt

¼ teaspoon freshly ground black pepper

1½ tablespoons best-possible olive oil

FISH

1 Arctic char fillet (about 12 ounces and ¾ inch thick at the thick end)

1 teaspoon olive oil

⅛ teaspoon salt

Oven-Roasted Bass in Cream, Horseradish, and Caper Sauce

SERVES 4

4 black cod or Chilean sea bass
   fillets (4 to 5 ounces each and
   1 inch thick)

⅛ teaspoon salt

SAUCE

½ cup heavy cream

2 teaspoons grated fresh or
   bottled horseradish

2 teaspoons drained capers

2 teaspoons fresh lime juice

⅛ teaspoon salt

½ teaspoon freshly ground black
   pepper

1 tablespoon coarsely chopped
   fresh dill

This easy recipe is best with a flaky but firm-fleshed white fish, such as black cod, Chilean sea bass, striped bass, swordfish, or cod. I like my fish slightly underdone in the center (my wife, Gloria, likes hers practically raw in the center), and this recipe reflects my taste, but the cooking time can be increased as you like.

The cream sauce is whisked together in a few minutes. (About 2 tablespoons of cream are used per portion, about the equivalent of 1 tablespoon of butter.) The cream is whipped just enough to make it slightly frothy, the rest of the ingredients are added to it, and the sauce is heated in a microwave oven for 45 seconds to warm it before serving. This sauce also goes well with steamed or poached scallops or shrimp.

Heat the oven to 350 degrees.

Arrange the fish on a baking sheet lined with nonstick aluminum foil. Sprinkle with the ⅛ teaspoon of salt.

FOR THE SAUCE: Pour the cream into a microwavable bowl and whip it with a whisk for 10 to 15 seconds, just until it is frothy. Add the rest of the sauce ingredients except the dill.

Place the fish in the oven for 10 minutes, for a slightly underdone interior. Meanwhile, heat the sauce in a microwave oven for 45 seconds to warm it.

Place the fish on warmed plates and spoon the sauce on top. Sprinkle with the dill and serve immediately.

To see how it's done, go to www.surlatable.com/jacquespepin.

Salmon for Grandma

Shorey cooks this recipe, similar to a miso-glazed salmon, to please her grandma. Gloria likes her salmon really rare inside.

The marinated salmon steaks are placed in a cold nonstick pan and cooked, covered, on one side only. The steam in the covered pan cooks the salmon on top, so it doesn't need to be turned over. It will be very moist, soft, and pink inside, with a crust only on the underside.

The timing here is for medium-rare steak; adjust the cooking time if your fish is thinner or thicker than about 1 inch. Often the belly part of the salmon is thinner at one end; in that case, I fold it underneath itself to make it thicker. Adding raw sliced mild onions at serving time is unusual, but Gloria loves Vidalia onions, and the crunchiness of the raw onions works well in this dish.

The marinade can be altered, with less or more of each ingredient, to suit your taste, and the salmon can be marinated and refrigerated a couple of hours ahead of serving.

FOR THE MARINADE: Mix all the ingredients together. Put the salmon in a dish and pour the marinade over the fish, spreading it to coat the fish well. Cover and refrigerate. *(This can be done a few hours ahead or just before cooking.)*

At serving time, arrange the steaks in a single layer in a cold nonstick skillet about 10 inches in diameter. Cover, place over high heat, and cook/steam for about 5 minutes, until the steaks are cooked but still pink inside and the undersides are well browned and crusty. (Adjust the cooking to your own taste, if desired.) Place the steaks on a warm serving plate, sprinkle with the onions, and serve immediately.

To see how it's done, go to www.surlatable.com/jacquespepin.

SERVES 4

MARINADE

1½ tablespoons dark soy sauce

1½ tablespoons ketchup

1 tablespoon maple syrup

2 teaspoons hot chili sauce, such as Sriracha

2 teaspoons rice vinegar

4 skinless, boneless salmon fillets (about 5 ounces each and 1 inch thick)

½ cup very small diced mild onion, such as Vidalia or Maui

Fish Tacos

These tacos make a great lunch. I sometimes use corn tortillas instead of the wheat flour tacos; they are more assertive in taste and a bit drier. Sea bass is one of my favorite fish, but you can substitute tilapia, grouper, sole, or red snapper according to your tastes and market availability. As always, the important factor is freshness.

The fresh salsa from my supermarket's produce section gives great results. You can vary the garnishes at will; in addition to salsa, I usually add sliced mild onions, cilantro, hot peppers, and shredded lettuce. Avocado, grated cheese, chopped tomato, cucumber, and the like make great additions too.

One fillet of fish is enough for 2 large tacos. The fish could be grilled, but in this recipe it is seared in a very hot dry pan (cast iron is ideal). The tortillas are quickly heated in the microwave oven at the last moment.

Heat a large sturdy skillet, preferably cast iron, until very hot. Salt, pepper, and oil the fish fillet and place it in the hot skillet. Cook for about 1½ minutes on each side, until seared but still slightly under-cooked in the center.

Meanwhile, wrap the tortillas in paper towels and microwave them for 1 minute.

Cut the fish fillet in half, place one half on each tortilla, and add the garnishes to your liking. Wrap and enjoy.

SERVES 2

¼ teaspoon salt

¼ teaspoon freshly ground black pepper

2 tablespoons peanut oil

1 fillet black sea bass (about 6 ounces)

2 flour tortillas, about 8 inches across

GARNISHES

½ cup shredded iceberg lettuce

½ cup hot salsa (store-bought or homemade)

½ cup sliced mild onion, such as Vidalia or Maui

½ cup loosely packed fresh cilantro leaves

1 large jalapeño pepper, seeded and coarsely chopped (about 3 tablespoons)

Shrimp Rolls

SERVES 2

2½ tablespoons unsalted butter, softened

2 New England top-split hot dog buns (about 4 ounces)

8 pink shrimp in the shell (about 8 ounces)

⅓ teaspoon salt

⅓ teaspoon freshly ground black pepper

2 tablespoons minced scallions

4 Boston lettuce leaves, preferably organic or hydroponic

1 teaspoon fresh lemon juice

I learned to make lobster rolls at Howard Johnson's in the 1960s, and I have always loved them. I buy them from small roadside stands along the Connecticut shoreline and also make them at home. For a change, I decided to show Shorey how to make them with shrimp. Any shrimp can be used, but I like to use the local pink shrimp that I can get in summer in Connecticut and Rhode Island. I have also had pink shrimp on Amelia Island in Florida. These shrimp are large (about 16 per pound), have a softer flesh than most, are quite flavorful, and cook very quickly. Other shrimp, or lobster meat, or even cooked fish fillets, can be substituted.

The shelled shrimp are sautéed in butter and seasoned with salt, pepper, minced scallions, and lemon juice. I first place lettuce leaves in the opened toasted buns so the lettuce holds the shrimp and buttery sauce and keeps the bread from getting soggy. I like the buns we always used at Howard Johnson's—top-split hot dog buns, sometimes called New England buns or Philadelphia buns. These come attached to one another (usually about 8 to a package), so the sides are soft, not browned, like the insides of the rolls.

Heat the oven to 400 degrees.

Line a baking sheet with aluminum foil. Spread 1 tablespoon of the butter on both sides of the hot dog rolls and place in the oven to brown for 10 minutes.

Meanwhile, shell the shrimp and devein them, then cut them into 2 or 3 pieces. Melt the remaining 1½ tablespoons butter in a large skillet and cook until it is a hazelnut color. Add the shrimp, salt, pepper, and scallions and cook for about 45 seconds. Turn the shrimp over, cook them on the other side for 30 seconds, or until just cooked and opaque throughout, and take them off the heat.

Spread the rolls open and line each with 2 lettuce leaves. Arrange half the shrimp in each roll. Pour the pan juices on top of the shrimp. Serve immediately.

To see how it's done, go to www.surlatable.com/jacquespepin.

"The biggest difference between cooking with my mom, dad, and grandpa is the conversation. With my mom, I talk about life and my goals. My dad and I talk about things in the news, especially if they relate to math and science. My grandpa and I like to discuss school—and food!"
—Shorey

Seafood Bread

This is a great recipe to make for a summer menu; it can be assembled ahead and refrigerated until cooking time. It's a great party dish. You hollow out a country bread and make crumbs with the inside. Then you fill the bread with fish, shellfish, parsley, garlic, butter, and nuts, top with the bread crumbs, and bake. I use calamari, scallops, shrimp, and cod in this version, but the dish works with only one type of fish, like salmon, or one kind of shellfish, like shrimp. I have even made it with chunks of chicken breast. And I have used big, round, thick breads; baguettes; or individual rolls. The only real change is the cooking time, which has to be adjusted depending on the size of the bread and amount of filling. This is great served with a green salad.

The stuffed bread must cook for 1 hour in a 400-degree oven. That may sound like a long time, but the bread needs it—and it will not be overcooked.

Heat the oven to 400 degrees.

Place the parsley, garlic, and nuts, along with the salt and pepper, in a food processor and process until well chopped.

Put the shellfish and fish in a large bowl and add the garlic mixture, melted butter, olive oil, mushrooms, and scallions. Mix well.

Cut off a thin slice from the top of the bread loaf and reserve it for a sandwich. Using your fingers, remove the soft insides of the loaf. Process them to crumbs in a food processor. (You should have about 2½ cups crumbs.) Place the hollowed-out loaf on a large piece of nonstick aluminum foil and bring the edges of the foil up around the loaf to hold any leakage during cooking. Place on a baking sheet.

Spoon about two thirds of the fish mixture into the hollowed-out loaf, packing it tightly. Press about half the bread crumbs on top

SERVES 6

1½ cups loosely packed fresh parsley leaves

4 garlic cloves, crushed and peeled

½ cup pecan halves

1 teaspoon salt

1 teaspoon freshly ground black pepper

1½-pound mixture of scallops, shrimp, calamari, and cod, cleaned or shelled as necessary, and cut into 1- to 1½-inch pieces (it is fine if you have more of one type and less of another)

4 tablespoons (½ stick) unsalted butter, melted

½ cup extra-virgin olive oil

4 mushrooms, cleaned and coarsely chopped (1½ cups)

½ cup minced scallions

1 loaf ciabatta (about 15 inches long, 5 inches wide, 2½ inches high; about 1 pound)

of the filling. Pack the rest of the fish mixture on top of the crumbs. If there is any leftover butter or oil in the bowl that held the filling, place the remainder of the bread crumbs in the bowl and mix gently to moisten them. Press the remaining crumbs on top of the filling. Cover loosely with aluminum foil. *(The loaf can be refrigerated for up to 1 day ahead.)*

At cooking time, place the loaf, still covered, in the preheated oven for 30 minutes. Remove the foil covering the loaf and bake for another 30 minutes, or until crusty on top and cooked inside.

Cool the loaf for a few minutes before cutting into chunks and serving. Enjoy!

To see how it's done, go to www.surlatable.com/jacquespepin.

Poultry and Meat

Crunchy Chicken Thighs with Zucchini

SERVES 2

2 large chicken thighs (about 1 pound), preferably organic

1 teaspoon peanut oil

¾ teaspoon salt

¾ teaspoon freshly ground black pepper

1 firm zucchini (about 8 ounces), trimmed and cut into ½-inch dice (about 1¾ cups)

¼ cup thinly sliced (¼-inch) dried tomatoes

I love dark chicken meat, and Shorey's and my favorite is from the thigh. In this recipe, chicken thighs are cooked skin side down, covered, in a skillet for about 30 minutes. They don't need to be turned over because covering the pan creates steam that cooks the chicken through. To further help in the cooking, I make a ¾-inch cut with a knife along both sides of each thigh bone. Then the fat that comes out of the chicken is used to sauté the zucchini for just a few minutes. Whenever possible, use organic chicken.

Place the thighs skin side down on a cutting board and, using a sharp paring knife, make a cut about ¾ inch deep on both sides of each thigh bone. Season the thighs with ½ teaspoon each of the salt and pepper.

Heat the peanut oil in an 8- to 10-inch nonstick skillet. Place the thighs skin side down in the skillet and cook for 3 to 4 minutes over high heat, making sure that they are not sticking to the skillet. Then cover tightly with a lid, reduce the heat to low, and cook the thighs, covered, for about 30 minutes. The skin should be very crunchy.

Meanwhile, heat the oven to 170 degrees.

Transfer the chicken to an ovenproof serving plate, leaving the cooking fat in the skillet. Keep the chicken warm in the oven while you prepare the zucchini.

Add the diced zucchini to the skillet and cook over high heat for about 4 minutes. Add the remaining ¼ teaspoon each salt and pepper and the dried tomatoes and cook, tossing, for another 30 seconds.

Arrange the zucchini mixture around the chicken on the plate and serve immediately.

Chicken Suprêmes in Persillade

From turkey to chicken to duck, everyone at our house likes the legs best. But when Shorey asked me why the legs are usually moister and tastier than the breast, I explained to her that the breast is usually overcooked. To demonstrate, I cooked a chicken breast my way for her, and she loved it. The sautéing process takes only about 5 minutes, and then the dish is finished with garlic and parsley, called in French *persillade*, and some minced scallions. The parsley, garlic, and scallions can be prepared ahead and the chicken sautéed at the last moment, though after the chicken is sautéed, it is good to let the meat rest for a couple of minutes before finishing the dish. Make sure you serve it on warm plates.

Heat the peanut oil in a saucepan. Sprinkle the chicken breasts with the salt and pepper, add to the hot pan, and sauté for about 3 minutes over high heat. Turn the breasts over, reduce the heat to medium, cover, and cook the chicken for about 3 minutes; it should be nicely browned on both sides and cooked through but still moist. Place the chicken breasts on warm plates.

    Add the scallions, garlic, and butter to the saucepan and cook for about 1 minute. Add the parsley and water and mix well to melt any solidified juices in the pan, then pour the sauce over the chicken. Serve immediately.

SERVES 2

1 tablespoon peanut oil

2 skinless, boneless chicken breasts (5 to 6 ounces each), preferably organic

½ teaspoon salt

½ teaspoon freshly ground black pepper

3 scallions, minced (⅓ cup)

2 tablespoons coarsely chopped garlic

2 tablespoons unsalted butter

2 tablespoons chopped fresh parsley

1 tablespoon water

Roast Chicken on Garlicky Salad

SERVES 4 TO 6

1 head Boston lettuce (5 to 6 ounces), preferably hydroponic

1 rotisserie chicken (about 2 pounds), plus ¼ to ⅓ cup of the cooking juices

½ teaspoon salt

1 teaspoon freshly ground black pepper

GARNISH

¼ cup extra-virgin olive oil

⅔ cup sliced scallions

½ cup coarsely chopped shallots

1½ tablespoons chopped garlic (4 or 5 cloves)

One of my favorite combinations is roast chicken cut into pieces and served on a Boston lettuce salad topped with a bit of sautéed chopped onion and parsley and the juices from the chicken. I usually roast my own chicken, but when I am in a bind, I buy a freshly roasted rotisserie chicken. Dark brown, shiny, and juicy, the cooked chicken is perfect with my salad.

I wanted to show Shorey how to use the supermarket in the best possible way, and how you can transform an ordinary chicken, making it your own, with a bit of imagination and know-how. I demonstrated how to carve the bird into eight or ten pieces with kitchen shears and arrange these pieces on young, tender Boston lettuce leaves spread out on a large platter. Sautéing a mixture of garlic, scallions, and shallots in olive oil and sprinkling that on top gives the dish a personal delicious touch. This dish should be served lukewarm or at room temperature, not ice-cold.

Separate the lettuce into leaves and arrange them on a large platter. Using kitchen shears or a knife, cut the chicken into 8 to 10 pieces (that includes the backbones, neck, wings, etc.) and arrange them on top of the lettuce. Sprinkle the chicken and salad with the salt and pepper.

AT SERVING TIME, MAKE THE GARNISH: Heat the olive oil in a saucepan. Add the scallions, shallots, and garlic and cook for 1 to 2 minutes, or until softened. Add the chicken cooking juices and stir well.

Sprinkle the garnish on top of the chicken and salad. Serve immediately.

To see how it's done, go to www.surlatable.com/jacquespepin.

Curly Dogs with Pickle Relish

This dish goes back to my days of working at the Howard Johnson Commissary in Queens Village. The commissary turned out tons of hot dogs, among many other products, and I had fun preparing them in unconventional ways: sliced in stew with beans or in soups, in salads with a mustard sauce, or with cabbage. I do not remember exactly how we invented the "curly dog." It involved cutting the hot dogs in such a way that they curled as they cooked. Each dog is cut halfway through lengthwise and then with about 12 crosswise slits, so when it cooks in a skillet, it curls into a "dented" wheel. I knew Shorey would enjoy making curly dogs with me.

The relish I serve with the dogs is a bit tart and uses dill pickles because Shorey loves it that way. I like pork and beef hot dogs, but any hot dogs will do. Only one hamburger bun is used for both the hot dogs, half a bun for each curly dog to sit on, and the centers are filled with the relish.

With a sharp paring knife, cut the hot dogs lengthwise about halfway through the meat. Then make crosswise cuts in each one, spacing them about ⅓ inch apart and cutting about halfway through the meat; you should have about 12 cuts on each hot dog.

Heat the oil in a sturdy skillet. Add the hot dogs and cook over medium heat for about 3 minutes, shaking the pan so the hot dogs roll over and brown on all sides. They will start curling up into wheels.

Meanwhile, toast the bun until it is crusty.

Place a curly dog on each bun half, curling it into a wheel. Spoon the relish into the centers and serve.

SERVES 2

2 hot dogs

1 teaspoon peanut oil

1 hamburger bun (about 2 ounces), split in half

About ½ cup Pickle Relish (recipe follows on page 93)

Pickle Relish

Combine all the ingredients in a bowl. Cover and refrigerate until needed.

To see how it's done, go to www.surlatable.com/jacquespepin.

**MAKES ABOUT 1 CUP;
ENOUGH FOR 4 HOT DOGS**

1 dill pickle, cut into ¼-inch dice (about ¼ cup)

¼ cup coarsely chopped mild onion, such as Vidalia or Maui

¼ cup diced (¼-inch) tomato

2 tablespoons sliced scallion

1 tablespoon ketchup

1 teaspoon hot chili sauce, such as Sriracha

¼ teaspoon salt

¼ teaspoon sugar

"My favorite junk food is either Swedish Fish or packaged macaroni and cheese."
—Shorey

Hamburgers a la Plancha on Ciabatta Rolls

MAKES 2 SANDWICHES

8 ounces ground beef

2 hard ciabatta rolls (about 4 ounces each)

1½ tablespoons olive oil

¼ teaspoon salt

¼ teaspoon freshly ground black pepper

2 to 4 slices ripe tomato

2 to 4 slices mild onion, such as Vidalia or Maui

2 to 4 iceberg lettuce leaves

Ketchup, mustard, and mayonnaise, for serving

Shorey wanted me to show her how to cook *a la plancha*. That Spanish term refers to fish, meat, or vegetables that are grilled on a flat metal plate or griddle. I use a heavy cast-iron or aluminum skillet instead, but you can also cook these hamburgers outside on the grill.

I like relatively lean ground beef for my hamburgers, either sirloin or chuck. I serve them on hard ciabatta rolls, rather than regular hamburger buns. I cut them horizontally into 3 slices, reserve the center slices for something else, and sandwich the hamburgers between the top and bottom slices only. That way, the ratio of bread to meat is less and the hamburgers are not too thick to eat easily.

I lightly brush the rolls with olive oil and cook them to a crispy brown in the oven. I cook the hamburgers in a very hot skillet for about 1½ minutes per side for medium-rare, which is how Shorey and I like them. At the table, our favorite additions are iceberg lettuce, tomato slices, and Vidalia onion slices, as well as ketchup, mayonnaise (Gloria's favorite garnish), and mustard, Shorey's favorite.

Heat the oven to 400 degrees.

Divide the beef in half and shape into 2 patties measuring about ¾ inch thick and 3½ inches in diameter; set aside.

Place the rolls on the counter and cut each one horizontally into 3 slices, about ½ inch thick. Reserve the center slices for another use. Spread 1 tablespoon of the olive oil on a baking sheet lined with aluminum foil. Press the slices of bread into the oil, turning them so they are lightly oiled on both sides. Place in the oven and bake until the bread is crusty and nicely browned, about 12 minutes.

Meanwhile, heat a cast-iron or heavy aluminum skillet over high heat for a couple of minutes, until very hot. Sprinkle the hamburger patties with the salt and pepper and spread the remaining ½ tablespoon oil on both sides. Add to the hot pan and cook for about 1½ minutes on each side, until nicely browned and cooked to medium-rare (or adjust the timing according to your own taste preferences). Remove the hamburgers from the heat and let them rest on a plate for a couple of minutes.

Assemble your burgers on the rolls at the table, adding the tomato, onion, and lettuce and garnishing them as you like with ketchup, mustard, and/or mayonnaise.

"The least fun thing about cooking, in my opinion, is cleaning up."
— Shorey

Meatballs in Tomato Sauce

Every cook has a different recipe for meatballs. My wife, Gloria, uses three different meats—beef, veal, and pork—in hers; I use beef and pork in this recipe. She adds eggs; I do not. We both use mushrooms, onions, garlic, and bread, although she soaks her bread in milk and I soak mine in water. Most cooks bake or sauté their meatballs. I poach mine in chicken stock so the outsides stay moist and tender.

Shorey loves all meatballs: her grandma's, her mom's, her dad's, and mine. Sometimes I serve these as an hors d'oeuvre with toothpicks and a mustard sauce, instead of tomato sauce. You can serve this as a pasta sauce or in sandwiches.

FOR THE MEATBALLS: Put the bread in a small bowl and cover with 1 cup water. Let soak for 5 minutes.

Meanwhile, combine all the other ingredients except the chicken stock in a bowl and mix well.

When the bread is soaked and soft, drain it and press on it with your hands to remove excess moisture. Coarsely chop, add to the meat mixture, and mix well.

Press the mixture into a rough 7-inch square on your work surface. With a large knife, divide the mixture into 5 strips one way and 5 strips the other way, so you have 25 pieces. Using your fingers, scoop up each piece and form it into a ball, then arrange the meatballs in one layer in a 10-inch saucepan. Pour the chicken stock over the meatballs and bring to a boil. Cover, reduce the heat to low, and simmer gently for 10 minutes. Set aside while you make the sauce.

**SERVES 4
(MAKES 25 MEATBALLS)**

MEATBALLS

1 cup (1-inch) pieces bread, preferably from a country loaf

8 ounces ground beef

8 ounces ground pork

¾ cup cleaned and coarsely chopped baby bella mushrooms (2 mushrooms)

½ cup chopped onion

¼ cup minced scallions (2 scallions)

1 tablespoon chopped fresh parsley

¼ cup grated Parmesan cheese

1 teaspoon salt

1 teaspoon freshly ground black pepper

¼ cup dry white wine

1 cup chicken stock

FOR THE SAUCE: Heat the oil in a large saucepan. Add the onion, garlic, oregano, and sage and sauté for 1 minute. Add the tomatoes, salt, pepper, and the liquid from the meatballs. Bring to a boil and boil gently for 8 to 10 minutes.

Add the meatballs to the sauce, bring to a boil, and boil for a couple of minutes to heat through. Serve.

TOMATO SAUCE

2 tablespoons olive oil

1 cup coarsely chopped onion

1 tablespoon coarsely chopped garlic

1 teaspoon crushed dried oregano

1 teaspoon crushed dried sage

One 28-ounce can diced tomatoes in tomato sauce (preferably Italian)

½ teaspoon salt

½ teaspoon freshly ground black pepper

"The best restaurant I have ever eaten in was Paul Bocuse's restaurant in Lyon. My favorite dish was the lamb I had as an entrée."
—Shorey

Roast Pork Loin Back Ribs

I have made several types of pork ribs with Shorey (see Spicy Ribs for Shorey, page 100), but for this recipe, the easiest, the ribs are simply rubbed with spices and roasted at a low temperature. These are not baby back ribs, but regular pork ribs, which are thicker and larger. They are best served lukewarm, and they reheat quite well. They are especially good with mashed potatoes and a plain salad. The spices can be changed based on your taste preferences and what you have in your pantry.

I cook the ribs covered for the first two hours so they remain moist, then uncover them for the last hour to get a bit of a glaze on top. Although some recipes recommend rubbing the spice mixture on the meat ahead of time, I add it just before cooking, because otherwise the sugar and salt will dissolve when exposed to the moisture in the meat.

Heat the oven to 275 degrees.

FOR THE SPICE MIX: Mix all the ingredients together in a small bowl and set aside.

When ready to cook the ribs, pat them dry with paper towels. Rub them on both sides with the spice mixture and place them on a baking sheet lined with nonstick aluminum foil. Loosely cover the ribs with another piece of foil. Place in the oven and cook for 2 hours.

Uncover the ribs and cook for another hour. Let rest and cool until lukewarm, then cut between the ribs to serve.

SERVES 4

SPICE MIX

¼ cup (packed) light brown sugar

1 teaspoon smoked paprika

1 teaspoon garlic powder

1 teaspoon onion powder

1 teaspoon English mustard powder, such as Colman's

½ teaspoon cayenne pepper

½ teaspoon chili powder

½ teaspoon salt

1 rack pork loin back ribs (about 2½ pounds)

Spicy Ribs for Shorey

Shorey wanted to make something special for her dad's birthday, and he likes barbecued ribs. For this recipe, I showed her how to precook the ribs in water first (this can be done a day ahead). Then we made the glaze for them together, adding one ingredient, then another, until Shorey was happy with the taste.

The cooking broth can be transformed into a vegetable soup, a favorite of hers, and finished with vermicelli (called *vermicelle* in French, or fine egg noodles or angel hair pasta) and Gruyère cheese; see Soup with Vermicelle, page 33.

SERVES 4

2 racks baby back pork ribs
(about 1½ pounds each)
or 1 rack pork loin back ribs
(about 3 pounds)

6 cups water

1 teaspoon salt

GLAZING SAUCE

3 tablespoons ketchup

2 tablespoons hoisin sauce

1 tablespoon soy sauce

1 tablespoon cider vinegar

1 tablespoon maple syrup

1 tablespoon hot chili sauce,
such as Sriracha

½ teaspoon garlic powder

Lay the racks of pork in a large saucepan, Dutch oven, or large stock pot, cover with the water, add the salt, and bring to a boil. Cover, reduce the heat to a very light boil, and cook for 1½ hours, or until the meat is just tender.

Heat the oven to 400 degrees.

Remove the ribs from the saucepan, reserving the stock, and lay them flat on a baking sheet lined with nonstick aluminum foil. Strain the stock. You should have about 1 quart; if you have less, add water as needed. Freeze for use in soup.

FOR THE GLAZING SAUCE: Mix all the ingredients together in a bowl.

Brush the ribs on both sides with the sauce, using about two thirds of it. Place in the oven and bake for 25 to 30 minutes, or until browned.

Remove the ribs from the oven and brush with the remaining sauce. When they are cool enough to handle, cut between the ribs and serve.

To see how it's done, go to www.surlatable.com/jacquespepin.

Sausage, Potatoes, Onions, and Mushrooms en Papillote

SERVES 4

4 mildly hot Italian sausages
(about 1 pound)

One 10-ounce piece of kielbasa,
preferably Polish, cut into
4 pieces

8 small Yukon Gold potatoes
(about 10 ounces), washed

2 carrots (about 8 ounces), peeled
and cut into 3 pieces each

4 large pearl onions (about
6 ounces), peeled

8 baby bella mushrooms (about
6 ounces), cleaned

8 large garlic cloves, unpeeled

2 fresh thyme sprigs

½ teaspoon salt

½ teaspoon freshly ground black
pepper

3 tablespoons olive oil

3 tablespoons chopped fresh
parsley

Dijon-style mustard, for serving
(optional)

I wanted to show Shorey how to make a great one-dish meal for dinner, so I chose this one featuring sausage, potatoes, onions, and mushrooms *en papillote. Papillote* refers to a wrapping of foil or parchment paper in which meat or fish is cooked. This is a great dish to make for a party, as it can be assembled ahead, even the day before, and then placed in the oven an hour before serving. We use nonstick aluminum foil instead of parchment paper, and Shorey put all the ingredients in the foil well in advance.

The food should not be wrapped too tightly, so steam develops and keeps the food moist. This dish can also be made with chicken pieces or meatballs, other vegetables, or fish.

Heat the oven to 400 degrees. Cut a piece of nonstick aluminum foil 32 inches long by 12 inches wide and place the foil on a baking sheet so half of it extends beyond the sheet.

Place the sausages, vegetables, garlic, thyme, salt, and pepper on the foil on the baking sheet and drizzle with the oil. Fold the extended foil over the ingredients and secure the three open sides of the foil by rolling the edges over on themselves twice. Do not wrap the foil tightly around the ingredients; they should be loose inside.

Place the *papillote* in the oven and cook for 1 hour. Remove from the oven and let rest for 10 minutes.

Carefully open the foil; the food will be steaming hot. Scrape the ingredients and juices onto a large platter, sprinkle with the parsley, and serve immediately, with mustard, if desired.

To see how it's done, go to www.surlatable.com/jacquespepin.

Pasta and Quinoa

Fusilli with Chunky Fresh Tomato Sauce

MAKES 4 CUPS SAUCE;
SERVES 6

SAUCE

2½ pounds very ripe tomatoes

3 tablespoons olive oil

1 onion (4 to 5 ounces), finely
   chopped (1 cup)

3 garlic cloves, crushed and
   very finely chopped (about
   1½ teaspoons)

1 teaspoon herbes de Provence
   or fresh thyme leaves

¾ teaspoon salt

½ teaspoon freshly ground black
   pepper

½ teaspoon sugar

1 tablespoon tomato paste

1 pound fusilli

½ teaspoon salt

½ teaspoon freshly ground black
   pepper

½ cup grated Parmesan

This classic tomato *concassée,* a fast onion-and-garlic-seasoned tomato sauce, is cooked only briefly, really a matter of minutes, so it has a fresh, delicate taste. It's perfect for pasta, and it's also excellent as a topping for rice or with sautéed shrimp, scallops, or grilled or broiled fish, or even as a vegetable dish on its own.

The tomato paste adds color, texture, and flavor, especially useful out of season, when fresh tomatoes tend to be watery and bland. I suggest you use the paste that comes in a tube; you can squeeze out only as much as you need and then recap it so the remainder doesn't dry out; it keeps for a long time in the refrigerator.

FOR THE SAUCE: Plunge the tomatoes into a pot of boiling water for 10 to 15 seconds. Drain and let cool for a few minutes. Peel off the skin (it will slide off) and cut the tomatoes crosswise in half. Squeeze the tomato halves gently over a bowl, pressing out the seeds and juice. Cut the tomato flesh into ¾-inch pieces and put them in another bowl. (You should have about 4 cups.) Strain the juices over the tomatoes; discard the seeds.

Heat the olive oil in a large skillet or saucepan (preferably stainless steel, to prevent discoloration). When it is hot, add the onion, garlic, and herbes de Provence and sauté for about 1 minute. Stir in the tomatoes, salt, pepper, sugar, and tomato paste. Bring the mixture to a strong boil, then reduce the heat and boil gently for 2 to 3 minutes. *(The sauce can be used immediately or refrigerated until needed. It will keep for a couple of days.)*

When you are ready to cook the pasta, bring 4 quarts salted water to a boil in a large pot. Add the pasta, stir well, bring back to a boil, and cook for 12 to 14 minutes, until firm but not too al dente.

Drain, then return to the pot, season with the salt and pepper, and mix well. Divide among four warm plates (I like soup plates) and ladle the sauce on top. Sprinkle with the Parmesan and serve.

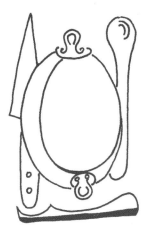

"If I could make a meal for anyone, it would be for my Papi, in thanks for all the great food he's made for me. I would make a roast chicken, salad, and pasta with garlic, butter, and cheese."
—Shorey

Spaghetti à la Bolognese

SERVES 4

SAUCE

2 tablespoons olive oil

1 cup diced (½-inch) onion

½ cup diced (½-inch) carrot

½ cup diced (½-inch) celery

1 ½ tablespoons chopped garlic

12 ounces ground beef

1 cup homemade chicken stock or
    canned low-sodium chicken
    broth

One 14-ounce can plum tomatoes
    in puree

½ cup dry white wine

2 tablespoons tomato paste

1 small serrano pepper, seeded and
    chopped, or to taste

1 tablespoon shredded fresh sage
    leaves

½ teaspoon fresh thyme leaves

¼ teaspoon salt

Claudine, Gloria, and I all make different versions of spaghetti Bolognese, and Shorey loves them all. My mother used to make it with leftover roast, finely chopped, and I have made it with crushed leftover meatballs or meat loaf. I like teaching Shorey how to be economical in the kitchen.

It is sometimes difficult to combine the meat with the other ingredients without lumps forming. To prevent this, I put the meat in a bowl, add some of the chicken stock, and crush the meat into the stock with my fingers. As the meat gets wet, it becomes a smooth mixture without lumps. Then I add it to the pot with the remainder of the ingredients and proceed with the cooking.

I cook the spaghetti and season it separately from the Bolognese sauce, then serve it with the sauce on top.

FOR THE SAUCE: Heat the olive oil in a large saucepan. Add the onion, carrot, celery, and garlic and cook for about 3 minutes.

Meanwhile, put the ground beef in a bowl, add ½ cup of the stock, and crush the meat with your hands to separate it. Put the tomatoes in another bowl and coarsely crush them with your hands.

Add the meat and stock mixture to the saucepan, along with the tomatoes and the rest of the ingredients, including the remaining ½ cup stock. Bring to a boil, cover, reduce the heat to low, and cook very gently for 1 hour. (Makes 4 to 5 cups sauce.)

MEANWHILE, FOR THE PASTA: When ready to cook the pasta, bring 4 quarts salted water to a boil in a large pot. Add the pasta to the water, stir well, and cook for about 9 minutes, until al dente (or to your liking).

Scoop out ¾ cup of the pasta cooking water and drain the pasta. Return the pasta to the pot, add the reserved cooking water, the oil, salt, and pepper, and mix well.

Divide the pasta among four warm plates and pour a good cup of the Bolognese sauce on top of each serving. Sprinkle with the Parmesan cheese and chives and serve immediately.

To see how it's done, go to www.surlatable.com/jacquespepin.

PASTA

12 ounces spaghetti, preferably imported

2 tablespoons olive oil

¾ teaspoon salt

¾ teaspoon freshly ground black pepper

½ cup grated Parmesan cheese

2 tablespoons minced fresh chives

Bow-Tie Pasta in Garden Vegetable Sauce

SERVES 4

⅔ cup frozen baby peas, defrosted

⅔ cup frozen corn kernels, defrosted

2 ripe tomatoes (about 12 ounces total), cut into ½-inch dice (2½ cups)

½ cup cleaned and diced (½-inch) white mushrooms (about 2)

⅓ cup coarsely chopped mild onion, such as Vidalia or Maui

⅓ cup coarsely chopped fresh parsley

1 tablespoon minced garlic (about 2 cloves)

2 teaspoons salt

1½ teaspoons freshly ground black pepper

¼ cup extra-virgin olive oil

12 ounces bow-tie pasta, preferably imported

⅓ cup grated Parmesan cheese, plus extra for serving, if desired

I always like to discuss the story behind a recipe, where it comes from and what it means. There is a small slice of life attached to recipes that matter, recipes with a history. These dishes are made over and over throughout the years; they are more than just recipes, they are a part of who we are.

In the early 1970s, while we were cooking at the home of Craig Claiborne in Southampton, New York, my friend the artist Ed Giobbi showed us how to combine cooked pasta with a summer tomato salad. The dish was what his grandma called *pasta a la primavera* when he was a kid. Sirio Maccioni, the owner of Le Cirque in New York City, made it a favorite at his restaurant, with all kinds of variants. I have included variations on that recipe in several of my cookbooks, but I wanted for Shorey and me to make our own rendition, using vegetables she likes and serving them over bow-tie pasta.

Other pastas—from penne to spaghetti to fusilli—can be used instead. Likewise, the vegetables can be varied based on what's available or in season where you live. For this recipe, I used frozen baby peas and frozen corn kernels; the goal was to make something delicious but also easy for a thirteen-year-old to prepare. The vegetables are combined in a bowl and seasoned with salt, pepper, and oil (this can be done ahead). Then, at the last moment, the vegetables are heated briefly in a microwave oven before they are tossed with the hot pasta and cheese.

FOR THE SAUCE: Combine all the sauce ingredients in a microwavable bowl large enough to hold the cooked pasta. Mix well and set aside.

When you are ready to cook the pasta, bring 3 quarts salted water to a boil in a large pot. Add the pasta, stir well, bring back to a boil, and cook for 12 minutes, or until firm but not too al dente (or to your own taste preference).

Meanwhile, place the vegetables in a bowl, season them with salt, pepper, and oil, and place in a microwave oven for 5 to 6 minutes. The vegetables should be partially cooked and hot, so they don't cool off the pasta.

Add ½ cup of the pasta cooking water to the vegetables and mix well. Drain the pasta and combine it with the vegetables. Add the Parmesan cheese and mix well. Serve immediately in hot bowls or on hot plates, with extra cheese, if desired.

To see how it's done, go to www.surlatable.com/jacquespepin.

Arugula Pasta Pesto

Many years ago, I bought arugula seeds in the South of France and planted them in my garden in Connecticut. Every year since then, I have been inundated with arugula. I unearth and throw away half of the plant every year and give seeds and roots to friends every fall. Yet it grows and grows, enough so that arugula is my daily salad from April to October. I have sautéed it and cooked it in soups, and I also make pesto with it.

The mini-penne called *mezze penne* is a favorite of Shorey's. I sometimes replace the arugula with cilantro, basil (for a classic version), parsley, chives, chervil, or sorrel, or a mixture of these, all of which are plentiful in my garden in the summer.

Bring 2 quarts salted water to a boil in a large pot. Add the pasta, stir, return to a boil, and boil, uncovered, for 10 minutes, until al dente (or cook to your own taste preference).

MEANWHILE, MAKE THE PESTO: Place the garlic, nuts, salt, pepper, and Parmesan cheese in a food processor and process for 15 to 20 seconds. Add the arugula and olive oil and process for 15 to 20 seconds. Scrape down the sides of the processor bowl and process again for 10 seconds, or until the mixture is smooth and creamy. Transfer the pesto to a large bowl.

When the pasta is cooked, remove ¾ cup of the cooking water and add it to the pesto in the bowl. Mix well. Drain the pasta, add it to the pesto, and mix well. Within a minute or so, the pasta will absorb most of the liquid.

Serve on warm plates with extra grated cheese, if desired.

**SERVES 4
AS A FIRST COURSE**

8 ounces mezze penne or other small pasta

PESTO

3 garlic cloves

⅓ cup pecans

1 teaspoon salt

¾ teaspoon freshly ground black pepper

2 tablespoons grated Parmesan cheese

4 cups lightly packed arugula, washed and coarsely chopped into 2-inch pieces

¼ cup extra-virgin olive oil

Grated Parmesan cheese, for serving (optional)

Macaroni, Spinach, and Ham Gratin

SERVES 4

4 ounces elbow macaroni

4 ounces (about 4 cups, loosely packed) spinach, washed

4 ounces boiled ham, cut into strips or cubes (about ¾ cup)

4 ounces aged Vermont cheddar cheese, grated (1½ cups)

½ teaspoon salt

½ teaspoon freshly ground black pepper

WHITE SAUCE

1 tablespoon unsalted butter

1 tablespoon olive oil

2 tablespoons all-purpose flour

2 cups milk

⅛ teaspoon salt

⅛ teaspoon freshly ground black pepper

continued

Like most kids (and adults), Shorey loves mac and cheese. We decided to add spinach, which is plentiful in her garden in summer, and ham. You can make the gratin without the ham and replace the spinach with Swiss chard or broccoli. I use only 4 ounces of macaroni here for four people because it expands quite a bit while cooking.

I use aged Vermont cheddar cheese for taste as well as color, and I assemble the gratin ahead and have it ready to go into the oven. If you prepare it at the last moment so all parts of the gratin are hot, reduce the oven time, or simply brown the gratin under the broiler for a few minutes. I cook the spinach in a microwave oven for a few minutes and mix it with the cooked pasta, ham, cheese, and seasonings in a bowl, then stir in the white sauce, arrange the mixture in the gratin dish, and cover it with the topping, ready for the oven.

Bring 2½ quarts salted water to a boil in a large saucepan. Add the macaroni, bring back to a boil, and cook for 6 to 7 minutes. The pasta should still be firm. Drain the pasta and rinse in a colander under cold water for 1 minute or so to cool it to room temperature, then place it in a large bowl.

Place the spinach in a microwavable bowl and heat it in a microwave oven for 2 to 3 minutes, depending on your microwave, to wilt it. Cool for 10 minutes, then mix it with the pasta. Add the ham, grated cheese, salt, and pepper and mix well.

FOR THE SAUCE: Melt the butter in a medium saucepan. Add the oil and flour and mix well with a whisk. Cook for 30 seconds, then

TOPPING

2 tablespoons grated Parmesan
cheese

2 tablespoons panko bread crumbs

½ teaspoon Spanish paprika

2 tablespoons extra-virgin
olive oil

add the milk, salt, and pepper and cook, stirring occasionally with the whisk, until the milk comes to a boil. Cook for about 30 seconds, then mix with the pasta.

FOR THE TOPPING: Mix all the ingredients in a small bowl. Arrange the pasta mixture in a 4-cup gratin dish and sprinkle on the topping. *(The gratin can be covered with plastic wrap and set aside until ready to cook.)*

At cooking time, heat the oven to 400 degrees.

Bake the gratin for 25 to 30 minutes, or until browned on top and hot throughout. Serve.

"My favorite meal would have to include at least three things—spaghetti Bolognese, caviar, and, most important, bread with lots of butter!"
—Shorey

Quinoa with Dried Cherries and Almonds

It's fun to expand Shorey's knowledge and introduce her to new, healthy, tasty ingredients. She did not know what quinoa was before we cooked it together. It is a five-thousand-year-old seed—not a grain—from a plant that looks like spinach. Gluten-free, extremely nutritious, and high in protein, quinoa can be used instead of rice, couscous, or other starches. It is great as an accompaniment to broiled, grilled, or sautéed fish, or sautéed chicken.

Melt the butter in a medium saucepan. Add the chopped onion and cook for 1 minute.

Meanwhile, put the quinoa in a sieve and rinse it under cold water.

Add the quinoa to the pan with the onion and mix well. Stir in the water, cherries, almonds, salt, and pepper. Bring to a boil, cover, reduce the heat to low, and cook for 25 minutes, or until the quinoa is tender and dry. Fluff with a fork and serve.

SERVES 4 AS A SIDE DISH

2 tablespoons unsalted butter

¼ cup chopped onion

1 cup quinoa

2 cups water

¼ cup dried cherries

¼ cup crushed almonds

¼ teaspoon salt

⅛ teaspoon freshly ground black pepper

Vegetables

Artichokes with Mustard Sauce

There is a whole strategy and routine to the cooking and eating of artichokes, and Shorey was happy to explore the process with me. First the tops of the artichokes are cut off and the leaves trimmed to eliminate the prickly needles at the end. The artichokes are then cooked in salted water until tender and cooled under cold running water. Next, I pull all the center leaves out in one bunch to expose the choke, scrape out the choke, and place the center leaves back in the opening. The artichokes are served cool, but not ice-cold, with the mustard sauce.

The sauce is a mixture of mayonnaise, Dijon mustard, vinegar, and water, with a dash of sesame oil, which gives it an intriguing roasted taste, but you can omit it if you prefer. Shorey has enjoyed these since she was three years old.

Cut about 1½ inches off the top of each artichoke with a sharp knife. Trim about ½ inch off the leaves to remove the spiny ends. Cut the stems from the artichokes, and peel off the fibrous skin from the stems.

Bring 3 quarts water and the salt to a boil in a large saucepan. Add the artichokes and trimmed stems and bring back to a boil. Place a small inverted lid or plate on top of the artichokes to keep them immersed in the boiling water. Reduce the heat, cover, and boil the artichokes and stems gently. Remove the stems after 15 minutes and set them aside. Continue cooking the artichokes for about 30 minutes longer (for a total of about 45 minutes), until a leaf pulled from near the base of one of the artichokes comes out easily. Drain off the hot water and place the pan under cold running water to cool the artichokes thoroughly.

Carefully drain the artichokes and, holding each one cut side down, press on them gently to remove excess water. Remove the

SERVES 2

2 large artichokes (about 10 ounces each)

1 teaspoon salt

SAUCE

¼ cup mayonnaise

1 tablespoon Dijon-style mustard

2 teaspoons water

1 teaspoon red wine vinegar

⅛ teaspoon freshly ground black pepper

1 teaspoon toasted sesame oil (optional)

choke from each one by pulling the artichoke open, grasping the central leaves with your fingers, and pulling them out in one clump, exposing the choke underneath. Using a teaspoon, scrape out the choke from each artichoke. Then place the clumps of leaves upside down in each opening as a decoration. *(The artichokes can be refrigerated after cooking, but remove them from the refrigerator 1 hour before serving to come to cool room temperature.)*

FOR THE SAUCE: Mix all the sauce ingredients together.

Put the artichokes on individual serving plates. At the table, spoon some sauce onto one side of each plate. Pull the artichoke leaves out one at a time, dip in the sauce, and enjoy. When the "meaty" interior of the leaves has been consumed, eat the artichoke hearts and the stems with more sauce.

To see how it's done, go to www.surlatable.com/jacquespepin.

Asparagus in Butter and Oil Sauce

It is important to teach economy in the kitchen, and preparing asparagus is a good example. It's important to know how to choose the right tight, thick stalks and how to peel the lower third of the stems so the whole spears are edible. Asparagus should not be overcooked, but it should be cooked enough to be soft yet still a bit crunchy. This recipe featuring asparagus in butter sauce is a delicate dish that is ideal as a first course for dinner or great alongside sautéed veal or fish. Asparagus is also good served cold with a vinaigrette or mustard sauce.

Holding each asparagus stalk flat on your work surface with one hand, peel the lower third of the stem by simultaneously rolling the asparagus over and peeling it downward toward the end of the stalk with a vegetable peeler. Then trim off about ½ inch of the base. Cut the asparagus into thirds, for pieces about 2½ inches long.

At serving time, bring the water and salt to a boil in a saucepan. Add the asparagus, cover, bring back to a boil, and boil for 3 to 4 minutes, until the asparagus pieces are tender but still firm.

Transfer the asparagus to a warm serving plate. Pour out the water, reserving about 2 tablespoons, and return the reserved water to the pan. Add the butter, oil, and pepper, and bring to a strong boil. Boil for 30 seconds to emulsify the sauce, then add the parsley, pour over the asparagus, and serve right away.

To see how it's done, go to www.surlatable.com/jacquespepin.

SERVES 2

8 ounces thick, firm, tight-headed asparagus stalks (about 10)

½ cup water

¼ teaspoon salt

1 tablespoon unsalted butter

1 tablespoon extra-virgin olive oil

⅛ teaspoon freshly ground black pepper

1 tablespoon chopped fresh parsley

Glazed Carrots

Cooks who use vegetables as a side dish for meat or fish often do not season the vegetables as they should. I wanted to teach Shorey that each vegetable dish should be able to stand on its own.

For this classic carrot dish, you can slice whole carrots or use, as I do here, baby carrots (preferably organic). The carrots are first cooked covered, in a little water seasoned with salt, sugar, pepper, and butter. When they are halfway cooked, the lid is removed and the carrots cooked until they are tender and all the liquid has evaporated, so the carrots glaze in the sugar and butter mixture. It's a great stand-alone dish as well as a good accompaniment for roasted meats or fish.

Put all the ingredients except the chives in a saucepan, bring to a boil, cover, and cook for 5 minutes over high heat. Uncover and cook for another 3 to 5 minutes, until all the liquid has evaporated and the carrots are glazed in the butter mixture.

Add the chives, mix, and serve immediately.

SERVES 4

1 pound baby carrots, preferably organic

¾ cup water

2 tablespoons unsalted butter

¾ teaspoon salt

¾ teaspoon sugar

½ teaspoon freshly ground black pepper

2 tablespoons chopped fresh chives

Stuffed Green Peppers

Stuffed peppers, tomatoes, zucchini, and eggplant are all part of our summer menus. The stuffing in this recipe goes with any of these vegetables. I always bring home the leftover plain rice from the Chinese restaurant we go to, which I use for this stuffing, or to make rice pudding. If you don't have leftover rice, combine ⅓ cup regular long-grain rice and ⅔ cup water in a small saucepan and bring to a boil, then cover, lower the heat, and cook for 20 minutes. You can also use cubed bread or leftover pasta instead of the rice.

I use regular green bell peppers, but poblano or long Italian peppers can be substituted. Although I like baby kale here, spinach—or even leftover salad—works just as well. The stuffing is made with ground beef, but turkey, pork, veal, or any combination of these is fine. The stuffed peppers can be assembled ahead and cooked at the last minute.

FOR THE STUFFING: Place the kale in a microwavable bowl and microwave it for 1 minute to wilt it. Let cool to lukewarm, then combine with the rest of the stuffing ingredients, mixing well with your fingers. Set aside.

Heat the oven to 400 degrees.

Halve the bell peppers lengthwise and remove the seeds and ribs. Arrange the pepper halves hollow side up and side by side in a gratin dish, then sprinkle with the salt. Divide the stuffing among them. Sprinkle 1 tablespoon of the Parmesan cheese on each stuffed pepper and drizzle the oil on top. Pour the stock around the peppers.

Bake the peppers for 1 hour, or until soft and tender. Serve with the pan juices.

SERVES 4

STUFFING

3 cups lightly packed baby kale (about 3 ounces)

12 ounces ground beef

1 cup cooked white rice

½ cup shredded Gruyère cheese

¼ cup chopped onion

2 teaspoons chopped garlic

1 teaspoon salt

½ teaspoon freshly ground black pepper

2 green bell peppers (about 1 pound)

¼ teaspoon salt

¼ cup grated Parmesan cheese

1 tablespoon olive oil

½ cup (salted) chicken stock

Cubanelle Peppers with Anchovies and Tomato

2 large, straight cubanelle peppers
(sweet Italian peppers; 10 to
12 ounces total)

20 small grape tomatoes (about
8 ounces), preferably a mix of
colors

1 cup diced (½-inch) stale
baguette (about 1½ ounces)

¼ cup minced scallions (2 or 3)

1 large garlic clove, cut into slivers
with a vegetable peeler

1 jar or can (about 3.3 ounces)
anchovy fillets in olive oil
(12 to 15)

½ teaspoon freshly ground black
pepper

1 tablespoon extra-virgin olive oil

1 tablespoon chopped fresh chives

Cubanelle peppers, also known as sweet Italian peppers, are long, narrow, mild-flavored, and light green. (Other peppers, including poblano and bell peppers, can be substituted here.) For this recipe, Shorey and I stuffed the peppers with cubes of left-over bread, grape tomatoes, garlic, scallions, a lot of anchovy fillets, and oil. I buy anchovies that come from the Bay of Biscay in Spain and France because the quality is exceptional. (No salt is necessary in the stuffing because of the anchovies.) This dish is good served lukewarm or at room temperature; it can be made ahead and then served at room temperature when needed.

Heat the oven to 375 degrees.

Cut the peppers lengthwise in half and remove the seeds. Place cut side up in a 6-cup gratin dish so they fit snugly and hold themselves straight.

Cut the tomatoes in half. Mix the diced bread, scallions, tomatoes, and garlic slivers in a bowl.

Cut the anchovies into ½-inch pieces. Add to the bowl, along with their oil and the black pepper. Mix well. Divide the stuffing among the pepper halves and sprinkle the olive oil on top and around the peppers.

Bake for about 25 minutes, until the peppers are soft and lightly browned. Remove from the oven and cool to lukewarm.

Sprinkle the chives on top of the peppers and serve, 2 halves per person as a main course or one half each as a first course.

Twice-Baked Potatoes with Sour Cream Sauce

SERVES 2

2 medium-to-large baking
   potatoes (about 10 ounces
   each), scrubbed

SAUCE

⅓ cup sour cream

2 tablespoons mayonnaise

2 tablespoons chopped fresh
   chives

¼ teaspoon salt

½ teaspoon freshly ground black
   pepper

Softened butter, for serving
   (optional)

Baked potatoes are easy and delicious, but large ones can take 1½ hours to cook. So for this recipe, Shorey and I microwave the potatoes for about 10 minutes, until almost cooked. (This is about the same time it takes my oven to reach 425 degrees.) Then we bake them for about 25 minutes in the hot oven. The skin gets crisp and nicely leathery during the baking.

You can microwave only two potatoes at a time in a microwave oven; any more will not cook properly. Some people recommend pricking the potatoes with a fork to prevent them from bursting, but this is unnecessary.

The topping is made of sour cream and mayonnaise, seasoned with salt, pepper, and chives; the small amount of mayonnaise prevents the topping from melting too fast and gives it depth. My wife adds butter to her potatoes in addition; you may want to sprinkle yours with extra salt and pepper. I cut halfway down the length of each potato and then cut them halfway down across as well, creating a cross. Pressing on the sides of the potatoes makes them open like a flower, and the topping can be spooned into the openings.

Heat the oven to 425 degrees.

While the oven is preheating, place the potatoes on paper towels in a microwave oven and cook on 100% power for about 10 minutes; they should be practically cooked.

130   *A Grandfather's Lessons*

Transfer the potatoes to a baking sheet lined with aluminum foil and bake in the hot oven for about 25 minutes. They should be leathery, crusty on top, and cooked through. Remove them from the oven and let them rest for 10 to 15 minutes to cool slightly.

MEANWHILE, MAKE THE SAUCE: Combine all the sauce ingredients in a bowl and mix well.

Cut halfway through the potatoes lengthwise and then crosswise and press on the skin so they open and some of the potato flesh squeezes out at the center. Spoon some of the sour cream sauce on top and serve, passing the remaining sauce and, if desired, butter, salt, and pepper at the table.

To see how it's done, go to www.surlatable.com/jacquespepin.

Mashed Potatoes with Garlic

SERVES 4

1¼ pounds Red Bliss potatoes, peeled and cut into 2-inch pieces

2 cups water

2 to 3 large garlic cloves

¾ teaspoon salt

2 tablespoons unsalted butter

¾ cup milk, or as needed

Mashed potatoes are the ultimate comfort food, and they complement most main dishes, from grilled meat to poultry, fish, stews, and roasts. I favor garlic in my mashed potatoes, adding it to the cooking water as my Aunt Aimée used to do for a delicate taste in the finished dish. I like my mashed potatoes silky and light, as does Shorey. I cook the potatoes in a small amount of water, so that at the end, the remaining liquid can be mashed into the puree; there is a lot of taste in that liquid.

I use a hand masher, whisking butter and milk in at the end for a smooth texture. How much liquid you have at the end of the cooking and how creamy and light you like your potatoes will determine the amount of milk you add. Pour in the milk ¼ cup at a time and mix well with a whisk after each addition. I prefer Red Bliss potatoes and whole milk, but you can vary the recipe based on your taste preferences.

Put the potatoes, water, garlic, and salt in a saucepan. Bring the water to a boil, cover, reduce the heat, and boil gently for 35 minutes, or until the potatoes are very tender. You should have about ⅔ cup liquid left.

Using a hand masher, mash the mixture into a puree. Add the butter and ¼ cup of the milk and mash some more. Add another ¼ cup milk and mix with a whisk to make the puree silky and smooth. Then add more milk if you like to get the potatoes to your desired consistency. If you are not ready to serve the mashed potatoes right away, spread 2 to 3 tablespoons of milk on top of the puree so it sits on the potatoes and keeps them moist on top; when ready to serve, mix in the milk.

Roasted Sweet Potatoes

I did not know sweet potatoes, or yams, until I came to the U.S. many years ago, but now I cook many variations of them, and they are a must for the Thanksgiving and Christmas holidays. Gloria particularly likes them halved and roasted in the oven (we cook butternut squash the same way). Sometimes I flavor them with honey or maple syrup rather than brown sugar and olive oil instead of butter. Shorey likes both sweet potatoes and butternut squash, and she wanted to know how to make this dish. The potatoes can be roasted a couple of hours ahead if need be. Line the baking sheet with nonstick aluminum foil to minimize cleanup.

Heat the oven to 425 degrees.

Trim about ¼ inch from each end of the potato. With a large knife, split the potato in half lengthwise. Cut a sliver from the bottom of both halves so they will stand flat. Using a sharp paring knife, crisscross the flesh about ¼ inch deep, making 5 or 6 slits in each direction. This will both help the seasonings penetrate the potatoes and make a beautiful checkered design on top.

Place the potatoes flesh side up on a baking sheet lined with nonstick aluminum foil. Brush the melted butter on top, spoon on the brown sugar, and sprinkle with the salt and pepper. Bake for 35 minutes until browned and well cooked. Enjoy.

SERVES 2

1 large sweet potato (about 1 pound), scrubbed

1 tablespoon unsalted butter, melted

1 teaspoon brown sugar

¼ teaspoon salt

¼ teaspoon freshly ground black pepper

Garlic Spinach with Croutons

I decided to show Shorey how to make this dish using garlic for flavor and croutons for a nice finishing texture. Baby spinach is the best choice for this, since it comes cleaned and ready to use. A 10-ounce container of spinach will seem like a lot, but as it cooks, it wilts to a small volume. First we pile the spinach in a skillet (not aluminum) with a lid, add a bit of water to start the steaming process, and cook the spinach covered for a few minutes, until wilted. Then we add garlic, peanut oil, salt, and pepper and cook the spinach uncovered for another couple of minutes, until there is no more moisture in the pan and the garlic cooks in the olive oil.

For the croutons, cubes of white bread are tossed with 2 teaspoons of peanut oil and browned in the oven for 8 to 10 minutes, until crispy. They are sprinkled on top of the spinach at the table.

FOR THE CROUTONS: Heat the oven to 400 degrees.

Cut the bread into ½-inch cubes and place them on a baking sheet lined with aluminum foil. Sprinkle the oil on top and toss the croutons to moisten them with the oil, then spread them evenly on the baking sheet.

Bake the croutons until brown and crispy, 8 to 10 minutes. Set aside.

FOR THE SPINACH: Pile the spinach into a skillet, preferably stainless steel, add the water, cover, and cook over high heat until the spinach has wilted and is soft, about 2 minutes. Uncover, add the oil, garlic, salt, and pepper, and cook, uncovered, stirring occasionally, until the water is completely gone and the garlic is frying in the oil, 2 to 3 minutes.

Divide among individual plates and sprinkle the croutons on top of the spinach at the table.

SERVES 2

CROUTONS

1 slice white sandwich bread (about 1 ounce), crusts removed

2 teaspoons peanut or olive oil

SPINACH

One 10-ounce container ready-to-use baby spinach

3 tablespoons water

2 tablespoons peanut or olive oil

1 tablespoon finely chopped garlic

⅛ teaspoon salt

¼ teaspoon freshly ground black pepper

Swiss Chard Gratin

SERVES 4

1 bunch (1 pound) young Swiss chard (with white ribs)

½ teaspoon salt

SAUCE

1 cup milk

2 teaspoons potato starch or cornstarch

½ cup heavy cream

½ teaspoon salt

½ teaspoon freshly ground black pepper

⅛ teaspoon grated nutmeg

1 cup shredded Gruyère cheese (about 1½ ounces)

In her restaurants and at home, my mother made gratins of potatoes, cauliflower, mushrooms, tomatoes, eggplant, and Swiss chard. I wanted to make this simple gratin of Swiss chard for Shorey. Back in my youth, the chard was always very large and only the ribs were used in gratins. The young chard available now is tender enough that you can use both the leaves and ribs, and it cooks in just a few minutes. I combine it with a white sauce, a simple mixture of hot milk and potato starch (cornstarch can be substituted). Adding cream gives the dish a wonderful taste, and the cheese makes a nice crust. This makes a great accompaniment to roast poultry or meat, and it can also be served on its own as a first course.

Heat the oven to 400 degrees.

Wash the chard and cut it into 2- or 3-inch pieces. Put 1½ cups water in a saucepan, add the salt, and bring to a boil. Add the chard and cook over high heat for about 5 minutes, until the chard is wilted and cooked but still a bit crunchy. Drain in a colander and rinse briefly under cold water to stop the cooking and keep the chard green.

Drain the chard well and arrange it in a gratin dish.

FOR THE SAUCE: Mix 2 tablespoons of the milk with the potato starch or cornstarch; set aside.

Bring the remaining milk to a boil in a saucepan. Stirring, add the slurry of milk and starch; the mixture will thicken immediately. Remove from the heat and stir in the cream, salt, pepper, and nutmeg.

Pour the sauce over the chard, moving the chard lightly with a fork so the sauce mixes in well. Sprinkle the cheese on top and bake for 30 to 35 minutes, until the top is brown and bubbling. Serve.

Fried Green Tomatoes

Fresh vegetables just out of the garden have been part of Shorey's diet forever. She enjoys carrots, radishes, zucchini, and peppers in full summer, along with plenty of tomatoes, from cherry to beefsteak varieties. Their season is short, however, and by the end of September, the nights are starting to get cooler in Rhode Island and Connecticut, and the tomatoes no longer get really ripe. This is the time to make fried green tomatoes. The slices can be dipped in milk, buttermilk, flour, or cornmeal; I dip mine in beaten egg and then into a mixture of stone-ground cornmeal and panko. I double-bread them for a thicker crust.

Place each tomato on its side and remove a thin slice from both ends. Then cut each tomato into 3 slices (about ½ inch thick).

Beat the egg in a shallow dish. Mix the cornmeal, panko, salt, and pepper on a flat plate. Dip each slice of tomato in the breading mixture to coat it lightly, then into the beaten egg, and return the slice to the breading mixture, pressing it into the mixture so it is well coated on both sides. Place the slices on a plate.

Heat the oil in a large nonstick skillet over high heat. When the oil is hot, add the breaded tomato slices and fry them for about 4 minutes on each side, so they are nicely browned and just cooked through but still a bit firm. Serve immediately.

SERVES 2

2 green tomatoes (about 8 ounces each)

1 large egg

¾ cup stone-ground cornmeal

¾ cup panko bread crumbs

¾ teaspoon salt

½ teaspoon freshly ground pepper

¼ cup peanut oil

Desserts and Confections

Blueberries in Honey Sauce

SERVES 4

1 pint blueberries

⅓ cup coarsely crushed cashew nuts

1 teaspoon grated lemon rind (use a Microplane)

¼ cup good-quality honey, preferably raw

2 tablespoons fresh lemon juice

½ cup sour cream

4 mint sprigs

Shorey is a voracious fruit eater—apples, berries, bananas, oranges, apricots. When she was five, I remember her eating slices of lemon; she loved the acidity. We made this dessert using blueberries, honey, and lemon, with the idea that she would enjoy any leftovers for breakfast.

We also created delicious instant "cookies," using plain sandwich bread, butter, and sugar (see page 145). Serve this dessert with the cookies.

Mix all the ingredients except the sour cream and mint together in a bowl and let the berries macerate at room temperature for 30 minutes to 1 hour, stirring the mixture occasionally.

At serving time, divide the blueberry mixture among four small bowls. Spoon about 2 tablespoons of the sour cream onto each dessert and top each with a mint sprig. The mint should be eaten with the berries.

"When Papi and I cook together, we usually make desserts. And they're delicious!"
—Shorey

Raspberry Jell-O with Strawberry Sauce and Blueberries

I first tasted Jell-O a few months after I came to America. I loved it then and I still love it. I often add fresh berries, cream, or a fruit sauce and sometimes crush cookies into the mixture. Shorey wanted to make this dessert for me. We used currant jelly here, but you can substitute strawberry, raspberry, or even apricot jelly instead.

Put the Jell-O in a bowl. Bring 1 cup of the water to a boil. Add it to the Jell-O, stirring it to dissolve the gelatin. Stir in the remaining 1 cup cold water. Divide the Jell-O among four glass or ceramic dessert molds. Cover with plastic wrap and refrigerate until set.

Meanwhile, remove the stems from the strawberries and cut them crosswise in half. (Notice that the tips of the berries are usually riper than the stem ends.) Cut the tip ends of the berries into fourths and set aside. Place the stem ends of the berries in a blender, add the currant jelly, and process until smooth. (You should have about ¾ cup.) Combine the strawberry tips and sauce in a bowl, cover, and refrigerate.

At serving time, spoon the sauce on top of the Jell-O and top with the blueberries. Decorate each with a sprig of mint, if desired.

SERVES 4

One 3-ounce package raspberry Jell-O

2 cups water

8 ounces ripe strawberries (about 8)

¼ cup currant jelly

½ cup blueberries

4 mint sprigs (optional)

Strawberry Shortcake

SHORTCAKES

1 cup (about 5½ ounces)
    all-purpose flour

2 tablespoons sugar

1½ teaspoons baking powder

¼ teaspoon salt

4 tablespoons (½ stick) unsalted
    butter, softened

⅓ cup milk

About 1 pound ripe strawberries
    (or substitute other berries)

Juice of 1 large lemon (about
    ¼ cup)

¼ cup sugar

6 fresh mint leaves

½ cup crème fraîche or sour
    cream

Strawberry stems or additional
    mint leaves, for decoration

Shorey adores berries, and I wanted to show her how to make a shortcake dough that would go with any berries or with other fruit in season. It is important not to overwork the dough, or it will toughen. I make it by hand here, but it can also be done in a food processor, with only a few pulses required.

The strawberries are sliced and marinated in lemon juice and sugar. I also showed Shorey how to slice the berries with an egg cutter. It is an easy technique that she instantly mastered. The green hull (calyx) of the berry can be used as a decoration—or use fresh mint instead.

FOR THE SHORTCAKES: Heat the oven to 425 degrees.

Combine the flour, sugar, baking powder, and salt in a bowl. Add the soft butter and mix gently with your fingers, crushing the butter into the flour mixture to incorporate it. Add the milk and mix briefly with a wooden spatula to combine. Transfer to a cookie sheet lined with nonstick aluminum foil. Using a piece of plastic wrap to prevent the dough from sticking to your hands, press the dough to form it into a rough square about 6 by 6 inches and ½ inch thick. Press your knife into the dough to divide it into 4 small squares; the squares should not be separated yet, just marked with the knife to make it easy to separate them after baking. Bake for about 15 minutes, until nicely browned.

Meanwhile, hull the strawberries, reserving 4 nice stems for decoration if you have them. Using an egg slicer or a knife, slice the berries. (You should have about 4 cups.) Combine the berries with the lemon juice and sugar in a bowl. Stack the mint leaves together, roll into a tight scroll, and cut into thin strips (this is called chiffonade). Add to the berries and set aside until serving time.

continued

When ready to serve, separate the shortcake into the 4 premarked squares and split the squares in half horizontally. Place the bottom halves on individual plates and divide the berries and juice among them. Cover with the shortcake top halves and top with the crème fraîche or sour cream, spooning a large dollop onto the center of each cake. Decorate each dessert with a berry stem or mint leaf and serve.

To see how it's done, go to www.surlatable.com/jacquespepin.

Instant Bread "Cookies"

Easy to make, delicious, and different, these are a lifesaver when you do not have any other sweets in your pantry. Slices of sandwich bread are coated with butter and sugar, cut into rectangles, and browned in a hot oven until crusty.

Heat the oven to 400 degrees. Line a cookie sheet with aluminum foil and spread the sugar on it.

Coat each slice of bread with 1 tablespoon of the soft butter, using ½ tablespoon per side. Press both sides of the buttered bread into the sugar on the cookie sheet, adding a bit more sugar if needed to coat the bread well. Trim the crusts from the bread and cut each slice into 4 rectangles.

Arrange the pieces of bread on the cookie sheet, place in the hot oven, and bake for about 12 minutes, until brown and crusty.

Stack the cookies on a plate and serve with fruit or other desserts.

MAKES 12 "COOKIES"

3 tablespoons sugar, or as needed

3 slices white sandwich bread

3 tablespoons unsalted butter, softened

Shorey's Raspberry Cake

SERVES 6 TO 8

1 all-butter pound cake (1 pound)

⅔ cup seedless raspberry jam

¾ to 1 cup sour cream

I decided to make a very simple cake with Shorey that she could duplicate for her mother, Claudine's, birthday. Claudine loves pound cakes, and she also likes the jam or jelly filling I used for the Christmas Yule log (*bûche de Noël*) I made for her when she was growing up.

I trimmed the cake, and Shorey made crumbs with the trimmings in a food processor. I sliced the cake lengthwise into four slices, using strips of wood (or cardboard) that are about ¾ inch thick on each side of the cake as a guide. The slices are coated with the raspberry jam and the cake is reassembled. Then the sides and top are coated with more jam and the cake is finished with the ground cake trimmings. Serve the slices with sour cream on top.

Buy a good all-butter pound cake and seedless raspberry jam.

Using a long, thin knife, trim the cake top, sides, and ends, removing about ¼ inch of the exterior, so the cake is smooth and straight. Place the cake trimmings in a food processor and process for about 15 seconds to turn the trimmings into crumbs. (You should have about 1¼ cups crumbs.)

Place two pieces of wood, about ¾ inch thick, against the long sides of the trimmed cake. Place your knife flat against the wood and, using it as a guide, cut a slice about ¾ inch thick from the cake. Set this bottom slice aside and repeat so the cake is cut into a total of 4 slices.

Heat the jam in a small cup in a microwave oven for 1 minute, then stir with a whisk to make it smooth and spreadable. Using a spoon, coat the bottom slice of the cake with about 2 tablespoons of the warmed jam. Place the second cake slice on top and coat it with more

jam, then repeat with the remaining slices of cake. Use the rest of the jam to coat the top and sides of the cake. Sprinkle the crumbs on the top and sides of the cake, pressing them with your hand. Refrigerate until ready to serve.

At serving time, cut the cake into 1-inch slices and serve each with a tablespoon of sour cream.

Grandma's Baked Apples

This is a classic recipe that my mother and aunt made, and my wife, Gloria, also makes it now. I usually use whatever jam I have in my refrigerator, and I sometimes replace the maple syrup with honey, sugar, or corn syrup. Most apples will work except for soft varieties like McIntosh or Cortland. Red and Golden Delicious, Pippin, and Gravenstein, as well as Pink Lady, all are good choices; although not always available, Russets are one of the best apples for baking.

I have a special corer that Shorey likes to use for the apples. I score the skin around the apples, about 1 inch from the top; as the apples cook, this upper portion forms a "lid." You can use slightly stale bread for this recipe; the bread under the apples gets soft and absorbs the juices the fruit releases as it cooks.

Heat the oven to 400 degrees.

Using a corer or knife, core the apples. Cut a slice about ¼ inch thick from the bottoms of the apples so they stand straight. Starting about 1 inch down from the top of each apple, score the skin all around. Place the slices of bread in the bottom of a small gratin dish so they fit snugly in one layer. Stand an apple on each bread slice.

Spoon the jam into the hollow apple centers and divide the butter among them, pushing it down into the hollow centers as well. Pour the maple syrup and water around the apples.

Place the gratin dish on a cookie sheet and bake for 45 minutes. Baste the apples with the juices and cook for another 15 minutes, or until they are very tender. Let the apples cool until lukewarm and serve with the sour cream, if desired.

To see how it's done, go to www.surlatable.com/jacquespepin.

SERVES 4

4 Russet, Golden Delicious, Gravenstein, or other apples (see headnote; 6 to 8 ounces each)

4 slices (about 1 inch thick) day-old baguette

6 tablespoons plum, apricot, or cherry jam

2 tablespoons unsalted butter

⅓ cup maple syrup

½ cup water

¼ cup sour cream (optional)

Meringues

MAKES 12 MERINGUES

5 large egg whites (see headnote)

1¼ cups sugar

Whipped cream, jam, melted
    chocolate, or ice cream, for
    serving (optional)

My mother used to make meringues for the Christmas holidays, so they are always very festive and special to me. Gloria, Claudine, and Shorey all love meringues. They are a great way of using up leftover egg whites, and they can be made weeks ahead. As kids, we enjoyed them served with apricot jam or topped with whipped cream. They are also great coated with melted chocolate, and a scoop of ice cream sandwiched between two meringues makes a great dessert.

I start with cold egg whites. The volume when beaten may be a bit less than if the whites were at room temperature, but the texture is tighter. I beat the whites on medium-to-high speed for about 4 minutes, until firm, add the sugar fairly quickly, and beat for about 15 seconds more to combine well. Some recipes call for beating the egg white and sugar mixture much longer, so it is very smooth, with no traces of sugar noticeable in it. Although that type of mixture can hold longer than mine, it produces meringues that are a bit chewy and elastic; the meringues in this recipe are very brittle and tender. To show different shapes to Shorey, I spooned some of the mixture onto the lined cookie sheet (see page 152) and piped the rest onto the sheet with both a star tip and a plain tip. While some recipes yield white meringues after baking, I like my meringues slightly beige, with a mild caramel taste.

To separate the eggs, I break the whole eggs into a bowl and then lift up each yolk with my fingers to ensure that the whole white is separated from the yolk.

continued

Heat the oven to 225 degrees. Line a cookie sheet with aluminum foil.

Place the egg whites in the bowl of an electric mixer and beat at medium-to-high speed until foamy. With the machine still on medium-to-high, add the sugar fairly fast (no more than 10 seconds) and keep beating for about 15 seconds longer to combine well.

Using a large spoon, scoop out some of the meringue to create 4 large oval shapes on the lined cookie sheet. Then, for a different look, fit a pastry bag with a star tip or plain tip, fill the bag with the remaining meringue mixture, and pipe out another 8 large meringues.

Bake the meringues for about 3 hours, until firm and light beige in color. Cool completely, then place in a container with a tight-fitting lid and store at room temperature until ready to use.

Serve plain or with whipped cream, jam, chocolate, or ice cream.

To see how it's done, go to www.surlatable.com/jacquespepin.

Vanilla Ice Cream with Mint and Lemon Sauce

Ice cream lends itself to all kinds of dessert combinations: It can be mixed or served with berries, berry sauce, chocolate or caramel sauce, nuts, and/or whipped cream, as well as combined with cookies. Or, for the ultimate dessert, sandwich ice cream between layers of sponge or pound cake, cover with meringue, and bake in the oven for a triumphant Baked Alaska.

Shorey adores lemon and mint, so I combined mint, lemon juice, and sugar syrup and added some banana slices to create a sauce that I served over vanilla ice cream. When I buy a pint of ice cream, I unmold it, cut it into fourths, place each piece on a sheet of plastic wrap, and press it into a ball, then wrap and return it to the freezer. The balls of ice cream stay free of freezer burn and are ready to be served, without the need for an ice cream scoop.

Using a Microplane, grate the rind of the lemon. You should have a good tablespoon of grated rind. Halve the lemon and squeeze it to extract ⅓ cup of juice. Place the lemon rind, lemon juice, mint leaves, and corn syrup in a blender and blend until smooth.

Peel and slice the bananas. (You should have about 1½ cups banana slices.) Place the slices in a bowl and mix in the sauce. Cover and refrigerate until ready to serve.

At serving time, divide the ice cream among four deep plates and pour the sauce and bananas over it. Serve with or without cookies.

SERVES 4

1 large lemon

½ cup loosely packed mint leaves

½ cup corn syrup

2 small bananas

1 pint vanilla ice cream

4 cookies (optional)

Chocolate, Nut, and Fruit Treats (page 158)

Chocolate, Nut, and Fruit Treats

MAKES 12 TREATS

8 ounces bittersweet chocolate, broken or cut into ½-inch pieces

8 raspberries

3 ripe strawberries, cut into wedges

About 1 tablespoon unsalted pistachio nuts

12 almonds

12 hazelnuts

1 or 2 sprigs mint

Shorey and I have been making chocolate desserts together since she was four years old. She likes chocolate in any form, from chocolate mousse to chocolate cookies, cakes, or truffles. These treats are great to make for the holidays, birthdays, and other special occasions. The recipe can be varied; for example, although we use dark chocolate, you could try it with white or milk chocolate. Or, instead of pistachios, almonds, and hazelnuts, you might want walnuts, pecans, macadamias, and/or peanuts. Rather than strawberries and raspberries, you can use blueberries or blackberries, as well as dried apricots, cranberries, or cherries.

We make our treats in very small paper baking cups with a 2½-tablespoon capacity; the bottom is 1 inch in diameter and the top is 2 inches. Of course, they can be made in larger paper or aluminum cups, but I find the small ones are quite enough for desserts, snacks, or treats.

Melting the chocolate in the microwave oven is foolproof and easy. Break the chocolate into ½-inch pieces and microwave it for 1 minute, then wait a few minutes before processing it further. Microwaving it for more than a minute to start will scorch the chocolate.

Put the chocolate in a microwavable bowl, place it in the microwave, and microwave for 1 minute. Let rest for 30 seconds, then microwave for another minute. The chocolate should be melted by then, but if it isn't, process it in 30-second increments, stirring after each increment, until it is totally melted and smooth.

continued

Arrange twelve tiny frilled paper cups (see headnote) on a plate and pour about 2 teaspoons of the chocolate into each cup. While the chocolate is still melted, arrange the berries, nuts, and mint on top of it in whatever manner you prefer—berries only or nuts only in some of the cups—and push down on them lightly to embed them in the chocolate. Refrigerate the cups for 45 minutes to 1 hour to set.

Peel the paper cups off the hardened chocolate and arrange the treats on a dessert plate. Keep refrigerated until serving time.

To see how it's done, go to www.surlatable.com/jacquespepin.

Chocolate "Rocks" with Hazelnuts, Croutons, and Cornflakes

When I was a child, my after-school treat was always a bar of dark chocolate and a piece of *ficelle* (a very thin, crunchy baguette), so, for me, the quintessential snack is bread and chocolate. When chocolate is king, Shorey is in heaven! So we made these clumps of chocolate that we call "rocks" by mixing chocolate with croutons, cornflakes, and hazelnuts. We have also prepared this recipe with Rice Krispies instead of cornflakes and used other nuts, but hazelnuts are my favorite. Berries or dried fruits—from cherries to raisins—can also be added. We favor dark chocolate, but you can use milk or white chocolate. We place the rocks in mini-cups or just on a tray lined with nonstick aluminum foil.

Here, we melt the chocolate in the microwave oven, but you can also melt it in a double boiler. The small croutons are baked in the oven with butter, and the hazelnuts are roasted to intensify their taste.

The proportions of chocolate to nuts, bread, and cornflakes can vary, as some people like these with more chocolate and other prefer them with more bread, nuts, or cereal.

Heat the oven to 400 degrees.

Put the hazelnuts in a small pan and roast for 8 to 10 minutes; remove from the oven. When the nuts are cool enough to handle, rub them together in paper towels to remove most of the skins, discard the skins, and place the nuts in a bowl.

continued

MAKES ABOUT 30 TREATS

¾ cup hazelnuts

1 tablespoon unsalted butter

1 slice thin white sandwich bread, cut into small (about ¼-inch) dice (about ¾ cup)

1 pound bittersweet chocolate, cut into 1-inch pieces

1½ cups cornflakes

Meanwhile, put the butter on a cookie sheet lined with aluminum foil and heat in the oven for a minute or so to melt the butter. Toss the bread with the melted butter and place in the oven to brown for 8 to 9 minutes. Transfer to a bowl.

Place the chocolate in a microwavable bowl and place it in the microwave for 1 minute. Wait about 30 seconds, then microwave for another minute. Wait 10 seconds and microwave for another minute. Stir the chocolate with a rubber spatula; it should be smooth and totally liquefied. If it is not completely melted, process for another 30 seconds at a time, stirring between increments, until it is smooth. (You will have about 1¾ cups melted chocolate.)

Combine about ½ cup of the melted chocolate with the bread and another ½ cup of the melted chocolate with the hazelnuts, mixing well. Place the cornflakes in a bowl and combine with the remaining melted chocolate, mixing well. Spoon about 2 tablespoons each of the mixtures into mini-cups or onto a tray lined with aluminum foil. (You should have a total of about 30 "rocks.")

Place the rocks in the refrigerator for a couple of hours, until well set. Then transfer to a plastic container with a tight-fitting lid or a zip-lock bag and store in your pantry, if it's not too hot, the refrigerator, or the freezer.

"My favorite thing to make
is always dessert."
—Shorey

Chocolate Goblets

These chocolate goblets are great fun to make, and since chocolate is one of Shorey's preferred foods, we had to prepare them together. I inflate latex balloons until they are about 5 inches in diameter and seal them, then dip the bases of the balloons in melted chocolate and set them on a tray lined with foil. The chocolate accumulates at the bottom of the balloons and forms a stable base. After an hour or so in the refrigerator, the chocolate hardens enough so that the balloons can be deflated and removed, yielding beautiful goblets, to be filled with ice cream, berries, whipped cream, fruit salad, or custard.

Although the chocolate goblets weigh only about an ounce each, you need extra chocolate for dipping the balloons. The leftover chocolate can be enjoyed on its own or reused later. The goblets can be kept at room temperature in a container with a tight-fitting lid or can be frozen. I prefer to use bittersweet chocolate for these, but any chocolate, from white to milk, or a mixture of chocolates, can be used.

Cut the chocolate into ½- to 1-inch pieces and put it in a microwavable bowl. Microwave for about 1 minute, then let rest for about 30 seconds. Continue microwaving the chocolate for 30 seconds at a time, stirring between increments, until it is melted.

Inflate the balloons to about 5 inches in diameter and knot the ends. Dip the bottom of each balloon into the chocolate, twisting it around to create a base about 3 inches high, and place on a tray lined with aluminum foil. Refrigerate the balloons for 1 hour. Cool the leftover chocolate and eat it or store it for later use.

continued

MAKES 4 GOBLETS

10 ounces bittersweet chocolate (see headnote)

4 latex balloons (about 12 inches long)

Prick the balloons or unknot them to deflate them, then gently pry them away from the chocolate goblets. Refrigerate, freeze, or store at room temperature in a tightly sealed container until ready to use.

To see how it's done, go to www.surlatable.com/jacquespepin.

Caramel Flan

One of the first desserts I remember is my mother's *flan au caramel,* which is usually called *crème caramel* in French restaurants, or, in English, caramel custard. The flan was a staple in the small restaurants that she ran, where she made it individually or in a large gratin dish from which she dished out portions. The Spanish call this dessert *flan* as well, and my wife, Gloria, with her Cuban–Puerto Rican heritage, was very familiar with it when we first met. Shorey has enjoyed flan from age two or three, and she especially likes the version I make using some condensed milk, as it is often prepared in Spanish-speaking countries. No sugar is added to the mixture because the condensed milk is very sweet; add about ⅓ cup sugar if you make it with regular milk.

I make individual custards in small Pyrex custard cups, but any small molds will work. I use 1¼ cups whole milk and ¾ cup condensed milk. My wife enjoys the leftover condensed milk in her coffee. I cook the flan at a relatively low temperature for a long time, which produces a very smooth, creamy custard.

Heat the oven to 325 degrees.

FOR THE CARAMEL: Have four ¾-cup Pyrex custard cups or other small molds ready. Combine the sugar and water in a small saucepan; bring to a boil, and boil for 3½ to 4 minutes, until the mixture turns into a nice golden brown caramel. Immediately divide the caramel among the molds; it will harden in a few minutes.

FOR THE CUSTARD: Beat the eggs in a bowl until smooth, then beat in the condensed milk, regular milk, and vanilla. Divide the mixture among the molds.

continued

SERVES 4

CARAMEL

¼ cup sugar

1 tablespoon water

CUSTARD

3 large eggs, preferably organic

¾ cup condensed milk (from a 14-ounce can)

1¼ cups milk

1½ teaspoons pure vanilla extract

4 cookies (optional)

Place the molds in a large ovenproof skillet and add enough hot water to come halfway up the sides of the molds. Place the skillet in the oven and bake the custards for 1½ hours, or until the blade of a knife inserted into the center of the custard comes out clean. Remove from the water bath and let cool.

To serve, unmold the custards onto individual dessert plates, spooning any remaining caramel out of the molds. Serve with cookies, if desired.

To see how it's done, go to www.surlatable.com/jacquespepin.

Decorating for Fun

IT IS IMPORTANT TO PRESENT AN ATTRACTIVE PLATE, but this should never be done at the expense of taste. I do not fuss much with presentation; I like my food still hot and not handled too much, so it looks natural. Shorey loves to decorate a plate, and showing her a few garnishing techniques made us both happy.

Some of the garnishes, like the olive or grape "rabbit," can be mastered instantly, while others, like the tomato rose, take practice. Seeing these techniques in a video is the best way to learn them.

To see how it's done, go to www.surlatable.com/jacquespepin.

Above: OLIVE OR GRAPE RABBIT: Cut a lengthwise slice from one side of an olive or grape and carve a small triangle out of the slice. Place the olive or grape cut side down and make an incision halfway down at the pointed end. Insert the triangle so the pointed "ears" stand up.

Opposite: LEMON PIG: For a lemon pig, choose a lemon with a pointed "nose." Cut a little wedge from the nose to create a tongue. Cut ears on each side of the lemon. Make a hole on each side of the nose and insert 2 black peppercorns for the eyes.

Left: LION-TEETH LEMON HALF: Cut off both ends of a lemon. With a paring knife, deeply cut "lion teeth," or a zigzag, all around the lemon and separate the halves.

Opposite: HEART-SHAPED CROUTONS: Trim a slice of white bread and cut in half diagonally. Cut each end to get a more pointed triangle, then trim each piece into the shape of a heart. The croutons can be fried in oil or butter or baked. For the presentation, dip the tip of each crouton into the sauce they will be served with or into melted butter and then into chopped parsley.

MUSHROOM FISH: Slice off the rounded top of a large firm button mushroom. With the point of a paring knife, draw the shape of a fish about ¼ inch deep on the flat of the mushroom. Cut away the flesh around the outline so the fish stands out in relief. Mark the head, eyes, and scales with the point of the knife. Trim the mushroom all around, then cut a slice off the top of the mushroom with the fish relief. Sprinkle it with lemon juice to prevent discoloration.

TOMATO ROSE: Remove the skin from a tomato in a long strip that can be turned into a rose; the sliced tomato can then be decorated with the "rose" for a salad. Beginning at the top of the tomato, cut away a slice, without separating it from the tomato, and then continue cutting a narrow strip, working your way around the tomato and using your knife in a jigsaw fashion to give a nice edge to the strip; it should be about 10 inches long. Cut another strip of about the same width and length. Curl the first strip on top of the tomato, which becomes the base of the rose. Roll the second strip into a tight scroll and place it in the middle to make the heart of the rose.

To serve in salad, slice the tomato into ½-inch slices. Arrange on a plate and sprinkle with salt, pepper, and a generous amount of extra-virgin olive oil. Decorate with the "rose" and serve.

ALMOND PASTE CARNATIONS: Mix ½ cup almond paste (found in most supermarkets, and also known as marzipan) with a few drops of red food color for the carnations, and ¼ cup almond paste with a little green food color for the leaves. For the carnation, roll the paste into a long, thin rope about ¼ inch thick and 12 inches long. Press one edge of the rope with a spatula to make it thinner. Using a fork, make ridges on the thinner side of the strip, then slide a thin knife underneath to loosen it. Fold the strip over itself in a wave-like pattern. Holding the carnation by the bottom, squeeze firmly to open the carnation into a beautiful flower. Roll out the green paste and make a couple of lozenges or triangle-shaped leaves. Mark veins in the leaves with your knife. Place the leaves around the flowers.

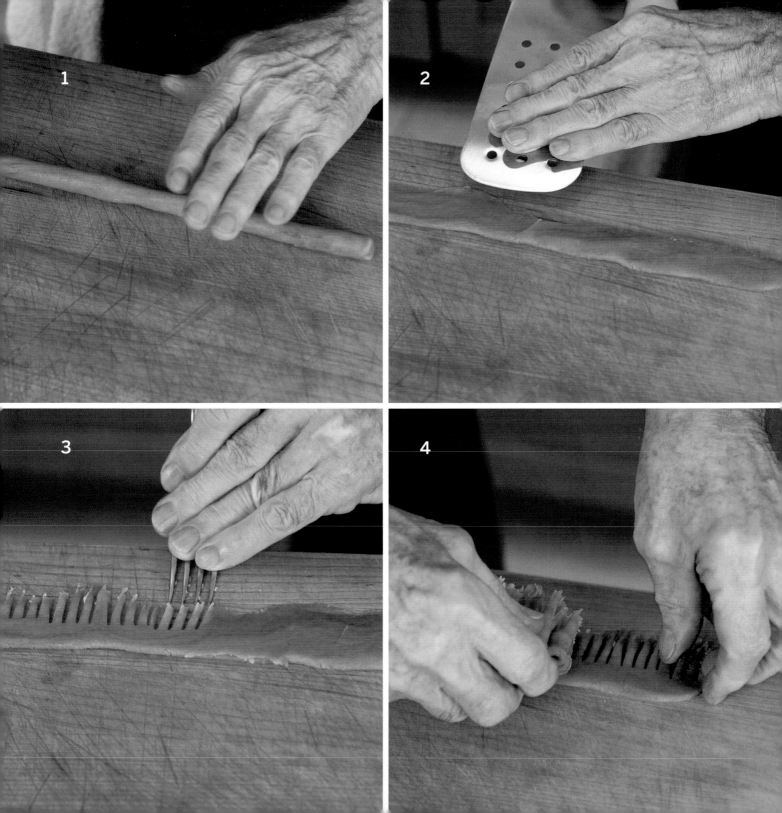

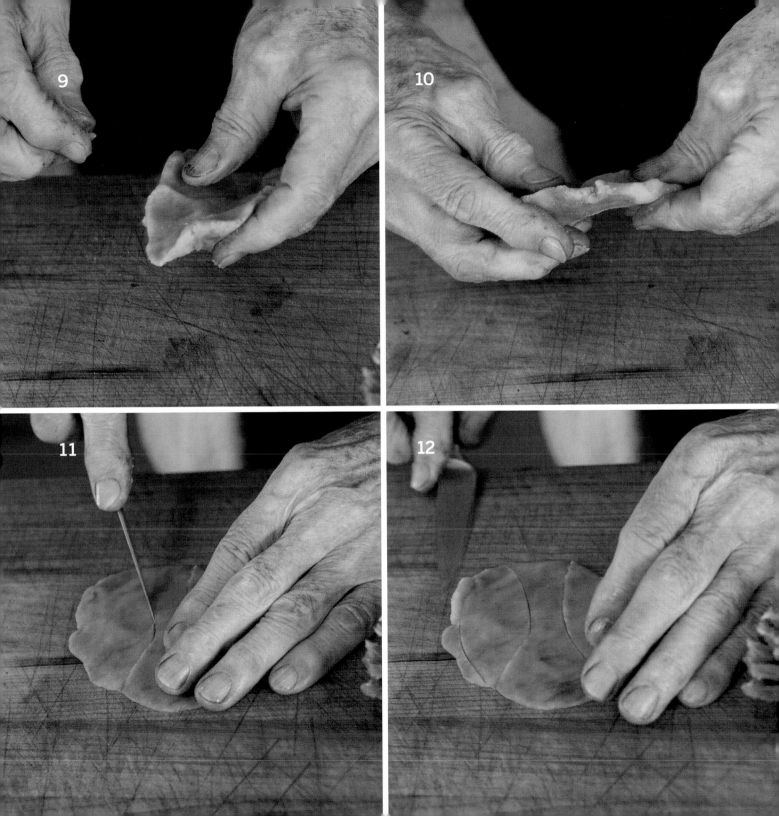

ALMOND PASTE ROSE: Shape a small piece of the almond paste into a cone to make the heart of the rose. Flatten one edge of another piece of almond paste with the tip of your finger or a spatula. Lift it and roll it around the cone. Roll another almond paste piece flat to make another petal and roll it around the flower bud. Keep adding petals to build the rose, turning the petal edges outward, until the rose is finished.

Index

Note: Page references in *italics* indicate photographs.

bread(s) (*continued*)
    making bread crumbs from, 65
    mushroom and scallop toasts, 68
    radis au beurre (radishes with butter), *16*, 17
    reheating, 65
    seafood, 80–81, *81*
    toasted baguette slices, 64
    see also croutons
butter
    and lemon, lemon sole with, 70, *71*
    and oil sauce, asparagus in, *124*, 125
    radishes with (radis au beurre), *16*, 17

C

cake, raspberry, Shorey's, 146–48, *148*
caper(s)
    cream, and horseradish sauce, oven-roasted bass in, 74, *75*
    sauce, fish fillets in, 69
caramel flan, 171–75, *174*
carnation flower garnish made from almond paste, 184, *184–87*
carrots
    glazed, 126
    rice paper vegetable rolls, 58–59, *59*
    sausage, potatoes, onions, and mushrooms en papillote, 102, *103*
caviar, salmon (or trout), deviled eggs with, 20–22, *21*

cheddar
    croque Shorey, 56
    English muffin pizzas, 61
    grilled cheese sandwiches, 57
    macaroni, spinach, and ham gratin, 114–16, *115*
    mini–sweet pepper treats, 18–19
cheese
    avocado, tomato, and mozzarella salad, 34
    chicken grits soup and chicken salad, *42–43*, 44–45
    cottage, pancakes with blueberries, 50, *51*
    croque Shorey, 56
    deviled eggs with salmon (or trout) caviar, 20–22, *21*
    English muffin pizzas, 61
    and herbs, fried eggs sunny-side up with, 48
    hummus with feta and sunflower seeds, 14, *15*
    macaroni, spinach, and ham gratin, 114–16, *115*
    mini–sweet pepper treats, 18–19
    sandwiches, grilled, 57
    soufflé/flan, easy, *52*, 53
    soup with vermicelle, *32*, 33
    stuffed green peppers, 127
    Swiss chard gratin, 136
    tortilla pizzas, 60
cherries, dried, and almonds, quinoa with, 117
chicken
    grits soup and chicken salad, *42–43*, 44–45
    roast, on garlicky salad, 88, *89*

    salad and chicken grits soup, *42–43*, 44–45
    suprêmes in persillade, *86*, 87
    thighs, crunchy, with zucchini, 84, *85*
Chilean sea bass, as substitute in oven-roasted bass in cream, horseradish, and caper sauce, 74
chives
    fried eggs sunny-side up with cheese and herbs, 48
    sushi salmon cubes, 26, *27*
chocolate
    goblets, 166–70, *168–70*
    nut, and fruit treats, *156–57*, 158–62
    "rocks" with hazelnuts, croutons, and cornflakes, 163–65, *164*
cilantro
    fish tacos, 77
    marinated Chinese mushroom salad, 38
cod
    fish fillets in caper sauce, 69
    seafood bread, 80–81, *81*
    as substitute in oven-roasted bass in cream, horseradish, and caper sauce, 74
"cookies," instant bread, 145, *145*
corn, in bow-tie pasta in garden vegetable sauce, 110–12, *111*
cornflakes, hazelnuts, and croutons, chocolate "rocks" with, 163–65, *164*
cornmeal, in fried green tomatoes, 137

fish (*continued*)
    oven-roasted bass in cream, horseradish, and caper sauce, 74, *75*
    salmon for grandma, 76
    seafood bread, 80–81, *81*
    sushi salmon cubes, 26, *27*
    tacos, 77
    see also anchovy(ies)
fish garnish made from mushrooms, 182, *182*
flan, caramel, 171–75, *174*
flan/soufflé, easy cheese, 52, 53
flounder, as substitute in lemon sole with butter and lemon, 70
fluke, as substitute in lemon sole with butter and lemon, 70
fried eggs sunny-side up with cheese and herbs, 48
fried green tomatoes, 137
fruit
    chocolate, and nut treats, *156–57, 158–62*
    see also specific fruits
fusilli with chunky fresh tomato sauce, 106–7

G

garlic
    arugula pesto, 113
    chicken suprêmes in persillade, *86*, 87
    mashed potatoes with, 132
    roast chicken on garlicky salad, 88, *89*
    spinach with croutons, *134*, 135
glazed carrots, 126

grains
    quinoa with dried cherries and almonds, 117
    stuffed green peppers, 127
grandma's baked apples, 149
grape rabbit garnish, creating, 178, *178*
greens
    salad vinaigrette, 41
    soup with vermicelle, *32*, 33
    stuffed green peppers, 127
    Swiss chard gratin, 136
    see also lettuce; spinach
green tomatoes, fried, 137
grilled cheese sandwiches, 57
grits chicken soup and chicken salad, *42–43*, 44–45
grouper, in fish tacos, 77
Gruyère
    chicken grits soup and chicken salad, *42–43*, 44–45
    soup with vermicelle, *32*, 33
    stuffed green peppers, 127
    Swiss chard gratin, 136
    tortilla pizzas, 60

H

ham
    English muffin pizzas, 61
    macaroni, and spinach gratin, 114–16, *115*
hamburgers a la plancha on ciabatta rolls, 94–95
hazelnuts
    chocolate, nut, and fruit treats, *156–57, 158–62*
    croutons, and cornflakes, chocolate "rocks" with, 163–65, *164*

heart-shaped crouton garnish, 180, *181*
hors d'oeuvres
    deviled eggs with salmon (or trout) caviar, 20–22, *21*
    hot pâté in puff pastry, 23–25, *24*
    hummus with feta and sunflower seeds, 14, *15*
    mini–sweet pepper treats, 18–19
    radis au beurre (radishes with butter), *16*, 17
    sushi salmon cubes, 26, *27*
horseradish, cream, and caper sauce, oven-roasted bass in, 74, *75*
hot dogs. *See* curly dogs
hot pâté in puff pastry, 23–25, *24*
hummus with feta and sunflower seeds, 14, *15*

I

ice cream, vanilla, with mint and lemon sauce, 155
instant bread "cookies," 145, *145*

J

Jell-O, raspberry, with strawberry sauce and blueberries, 141

K

kale, in stuffed green peppers, 127

L

lemon
    and butter, lemon sole with, 70, *71*
    half lion-teeth garnish, creating, 180, *180*
    and mint sauce, vanilla ice cream with, 155

Menu for
Mom 🖤

Wine:
Rosé de
Provence

Artichokes
with Mustard
Sauce
~
Lemon Sole with
Butter and Capers
~
Garlic Spinach
with Croutons
~
Salade
Vinaigrette
~
Shorey's
Raspberry
Cake